RAILWAY NOSTALGIA
AROUND BEDFORDSHIRE

Jubilee 4-6-0 No. 5598 "Basutoland" passes Chiltern Green on
Thursday 13 July 1939 with the 15.35 express from St Pancras to
Bradford. (*H.C. Casserley*)

Front endpaper (left)
The preserved Jones Goods 4-6-0 No. 103 leaves Old Warden Tunnel during filming of sequences for the feature film
Those Magnificent Men in Their Flying Machines in May 1964. (*F.G. Cockman*)

Un-rebuilt WC Pacific No. 34006 "Bude" leaves Bedford Midland Road on Saturday 11 May 1963 with a joint LCGB/SLS special from
St Pancras to Derby. (*B. Wheeler*)

Front endpaper (right)
Nameplate of un-rebuilt Patriot 4-6-0 No. 45516, photographed on Bedford Shed. (*Brian Lockey*)

Title page
'Flying Scotsman' breasts Sharnbrook Summit with a north-bound special excursion train on Saturday 18 November 1967. (*J.D. Lyne*)

Rear endpaper (left)
Two 0-4-0 saddle tanks from the fascinating stud of industrial locomotives that used to work for the Wellingborough Iron Co. Above is
3 ft. 3 in. gauge Bagnall No. 10 of 1918, photographed on Saturday 4 November 1933, and below is standard gauge Hudswell Clarke &
Rodgers No. 6 of 1876, photographed on Saturday 9 March 1935. (*R.G. Jarvis*)

Rear endpaper (right)
Superheated Precursor 4-4-0 No. 25304 "Greyhound", leaves Sandy with a goods train for Bedford on Saturday 1 May 1937. (*Les Hanson*)

Frontispiece. Volcano! Positively erupting out of the Royston line sidings at Hitchin on 2 March 1963 is New England shed's 9F No. 92182. Despite its 10 driving wheels, the loco is having severe trouble getting its heavy load on the move over the points on this frosty winter's morning, and although the sanding equipment is being used liberally, the plumes of smoke are the result of extremely frenzied bouts of slipping. Altogether No. 92182 took fully 20 minutes to get its train out of the yard and under way, an episode witnessed only by a handful of totally uninterested passengers on the platform, a few mickey-taking railwaymen … and the photographer! What wouldn't today's enthusiasts and steam photographers give to witness such a grand spectacle?

(*S. Summerson*)

RAILWAY NOSTALGIA
AROUND BEDFORDSHIRE

by
DAVID EATWELL

W. D. WHARTON
Wellingborough

First published in 1995 by
W.D. Wharton
37 Sheep Street
Wellingborough
Northamptonshire NN8 1BX

David Eatwell asserts his moral right
to be identified as the author of this work

ISBN 0 9518557 7 8

Designed and typeset by John Hardaker, Wollaston, Northamptonshire
Printed and bound in Great Britain by
Butler & Tanner Ltd
Frome, Somerset

CONTENTS

For Big Trev

ACKNOWLEDGEMENTS

Ever since the series of photo-albums on the Railways of Northamptonshire by Richard Coleman and Joe Rajczonek were published, I have been an ardent fan, so when I first thought I might be able to compile a sister volume on Bedfordshire, it was to Joe that I went with the idea. Not only did he show both considerable encouragement and enthusiasm for the project, he also communicated this enthusiasm to publisher Robert Wharton and, as a result, *Railway Nostalgia Around Bedfordshire* was born.

By its very nature, any compilation of photographs such as this is heavily dependent upon the co-operation of the photographers, and I have been most gratified that many of the top names in the field have allowed me to make use of their work. I am particularly grateful to those who entrusted me with their priceless negatives so that I could print them in my darkroom, and I hope they will think I have done them justice.

Where known, each of these great men is credited separately with his photograph, and many have kindly given up some of their time to check relevant captions, but all the way through the preparation of the text I have also received the most generous assistance from whoever else I approached, particularly: Members of the Bedford Branch of ASLEF, Robert Casserley, Fred Cockman, Gordon Eckersley, Colin Franklin, Chris Foren, Dave Hounam, Greg Howell, Lance King, Ray King, Jess Lay, Alan Ledwick, Dave Mills, John Parker, William Shelford, Peter Terry and the late Geoffrey Webb.

Over the years, it has been my great good fortune to have accumulated some very knowledgeable friends, and many of these gentlemen have unselfishly donated their expertise to help make the captions as extensive and informative as they are. Among the experts are: Malcolm Burgoyne, Ted Burley, Jack Butcher, Richard Crane, Bryan Cross, Bill Davies, Nick Pigott, Hugh Ramsey, Ray Schofield, Stephen Summerson, Robin Waywell and Geoff Woodward.

The most important printed references were: Various ABCs and Shed Books from Ian Allan, *British Locomotives of the 20th Century* by O.S. Nock, *The Hatfield, Luton & Dunstable Railway* by Sue and Geoff Woodward, *LMS Engine Sheds* by Hawkins and Reeve, *The Midland Railway, A Chronology* by John Gough, *Oxford to Cambridge Railway* by Bill Simpson, *The Railway Age in Bedfordshire* by Fred Cockman, *The Railwaymen, Wolverton* by Bill West, *The Rushden, Higham Ferrers Branch* by Peter Butler, *Steam Locomotives of British Railways* by H.C. Casserley and a host of railway magazines.

My publisher, Robert Wharton, and editor, John Hardaker, have both shown more than a fair share of patience and understanding during the preparation of *Railway Nostalgia Around Bedfordshire*; lesser men might well have given up on me long ago.

Last, but by no means least, I must pay tribute to my wife Joan, who painstakingly and laboriously made sense of my scribble, cleverly transferring it into comprehensible matter on her WP. Unfortunately, her well-meant efforts to initiate me into the mysteries of the machine were doomed to failure, and I am resigned to being able to operate nothing more complicated than a typewriter. Sorry.

To all the above, I proffer my most sincere and heartfelt thanks.

D.E.

FOREWORD BY O.S. NOCK

Having used many of David's fine photographs in several of my own books, I feel it is a great honour to be asked to write a foreword to *his* book, even though Bedfordshire in my case has always been, but for one memorable exception, a county for going through, rather than going to. From 1916 my parents lived in Barrow-in-Furness, and during my university days and for some time thereafter I was travelling from Euston by the West Coast Main Line, thus touching the county briefly at Leighton Buzzard. But my railway interests extended to the logging of many fast runs, and I was often through Bedfordshire, mostly at high speed. The first time I ever recorded a maximum speed of 90 mph was in 1935 on the Queen of Scots Pullman near Three Counties station. I was on the footplate of a Great Northern Atlantic and, apart from the sheer thrill, I recall it as very rough and uncomfortable – but that was the way of all engines of that class. On a sweltering summer's day we tore north through the county, covering the 16 miles from Three Counties to St Neots at an average speed of 83 mph. Since then I have clocked far higher speeds, some well over 100 mph, but that first occasion was a milestone in my life – and in Bedfordshire.

On many journeys through the county on Midland Scotch Expresses I was never treated to such speed as I experienced on the streamlined trains or even with the Pullmans, but I do have memories on the other fringe of the county which David covers, as he ventures as far afield as Bletchley in his book. A great friend, far senior in years to me, used at one time to live in the village of Middleton Stoney near Bicester. He was a keen railway enthusiast, and kept a log book which he bequeathed to me. His journeys on the Oxford branch of the LNWR from Bletchley, in the days when the Ramsbottom 2-2-2 engines (with their 7'6" driving-wheels) were the standard motive power of the line, make fascinating reading. His journeys to London had to be made via Bletchley or Oxford, and I gather that the former route was his favourite. He used the LNWR main line for his journeys to Scotland where he had some relations in Greenock. His log book does not extend beyond 1906, but it does include some notes on the earliest workings of the Whale express locomotives.

Territorially, the county of Bedford now briefly impinges on the West Coast Main Line from Euston to the north near Leighton Buzzard. The town itself, centre of a major road junction, lies about a mile east of the railway, and the station is in the village of Linslade which gave its name to the short tunnels cutting through the big hill just north of the station. When the London & Birmingham Railway was built, only two running lines were needed, and the Linslade Tunnel had a single bore with a handsome entrance characteristic of the other tunnel entrances on that pioneer railway. But when the widening of the line took place, two single-line tunnels were built on each side of the original bore, and the down main line went through a single bore. In travelling north from Euston, I had always been aware of this, but it was not until I came to ride on the footplate of a fast train that I experienced what it was like for the enginemen. With a large-boilered locomotive like a Royal Scot, entering that single-line tunnel at high speed was like hitting a solid wall of air. The down express I was riding had just been descending from its crossing of the Chiltern Hills and was doing around 75 mph, and as this was my first footplate journey, the fireman very kindly gave me a cloth to cover my head. Otherwise I would have been smothered with flying grit and cinders when we entered the tunnel. So much for Bedfordshire!

At the end of 1911 the Great Western Railway named the first of a new batch of outside cylinder 4-4-0s 'County of Bedford'. There had been many Counties before on the GWR, some named after Irish ones with which they had a traffic connection via Fishguard, but why Bedford, the only one of the 40 names on those 4-4-0s with which the Great Western had no physical or traffic connection? And then the Hornby model railway firm chose No. 3821 'County of Bedford' for their 'O'-gauge model. At home, our own model railway had not gone further than tin-plate track on the nursery floor at that time, and my son Trevor, then aged about eight, became very proud of his 'County of Bedford' which used to tear round the circuit at incredible speeds. I have always heard that the Counties were rough riding engines, yet that Hornby model excelled them all, and I often wondered if in real life they were ever as rough as that Great Northern Atlantic that gave me such a shaking-up when I recorded my first ever 90 mph at Three Counties on the 'Queen of Scots' Pullman way back in 1935.

Nock

I was fortunate to be able to show 'Ossie' Nock the layout of my book before his sad passing.
The above is probably the last he wrote on his all-consuming passion of railways. – D.E.

INTRODUCTION

Bedfordshire, as 'Ossie' Nock says in his foreword, is often regarded as a county for going *through*, not for going *to*, and go through it is certainly what some of England's earliest railway builders did – leaving much of their legacy for all to enjoy today.

Three trunk routes cross Bedfordshire – the West Coast Main Line out of Euston, the Midland Main Line from St Pancras and the East Coast Main Line out of King's Cross – and some fascinating cross-country lines once meandered here and there before Beeching set about the nation's railway system with his notorious axe.

All that now remains of the county's minor standard gauge railways is the Bedford to Bletchley line, and for that we have to thank the Bedford-Bletchley Rail Users Association, a flourishing pressure group which has seen a steady rise in the number of passengers using the line in recent years. At the time of writing, semaphore signals and hand-operated level-crossing gates are some of the delights travellers on this 'time-warp railway' may still admire as they ride the line, perhaps heading for a day's shopping at nearby Milton Keynes, to make a connection with an express on the electrified West Coast Main Line or, in the opposite direction, to connect with Thameslink and Midland Main Line services.

How much longer this charming route will retain such old-fashioned features (or indeed be allowed to stay open) remains to be seen. Should the worst happen, it is some consolation that photographers over the years have preserved it on film for future generations to savour, and much of their work has already been published. Perhaps more than any other branch-line in the area, that from Oxford to Cambridge (of which the Bedford-Bletchley section formed such a vital part) has often been featured in print, and for that reason it has not been so heavily covered in this book.

But it was not just the Bedford-Bletchley line that attracted serious photographers, for over the years they came to all parts of Bedford-shire (rather than passing through) and, alongside the natives, carefully recorded for posterity scenes of railway lines that have long since gone. The line from Leighton Buzzard to Luton (and Hatfield), the old Midland Main Line from Bedford to Hitchin, the contin-uation of the Bletchley-Bedford line through Sandy, and the Bedford-Northampton line through to Olney – all are covered in this book.

Although strictly about railways in Bedfordshire, the book's scope has been extended slightly beyond the county boundaries to include the branch line to Higham Ferrers. There are also glimpses of trams (actually street railways). It is perhaps not generally remembered today that trams once ran in both Luton and Wolverton.

Bedfordshire used to have many industrial railways, including those at Vauxhall Motors, the Stewartby and Lidlington area Brickworks, Leighton Buzzard Sand Quarry and Houghton Regis Cement Works: the special character of each is portrayed. None of these operations survives today (although preservationists have taken over part of the Leighton Buzzard narrow gauge system), but many of the locomotives that were used on them are preserved at centres such as Quainton Road (near Aylesbury) where steamings frequently occur.

Naturally, though, the greater part of the book is devoted to the main lines and their locomotives. Readers will have their own favourites, and I hope they will find them represented. Black Fives, Midland Compounds, and V2s; Coronations, Jubilees and A4s are all shown, together with a wide diversity of other types – little and large, ancient and modern – going back to the earliest days of photography.

No attempt has been made to show every class of locomotive, nor indeed every station, every signal box or every set of semaphore signals that ever there was in the county, and inevitably some features appear more than others. Sandy, for example, was frequently photographed, as were both Bedford and Bletchley: the number of pictures reflects their popularity with cameramen.

The intention has been to use mostly unpublished material, and in the main this has been achieved, but a few of the photographs selected may have been seen elsewhere. Overall, though, the number of previously published pictures is minimal compared with the new ones unearthed during recent researches.

Luckily for us, many top railway photographers stopped off in Bedfordshire and exercised their shutters on the county's railways, and their photographs on the pages which follow show how much was missed by those who merely passed through.

David Eatwell
Bedford

BEDFORD (MIDLAND)

A panoramic view of the Bedford Shed area in February 1952

1. When the official photographer climbed the coaling-tower to record the completion of Bedford Shed's new roof, the onset of diesel traction here was still six years away, and electrification not even to be seriously proposed for another 20 years.

In this wonderfully evocative view, eight locomotives are visible, most of them fondly remembered by Bedford loco-men. To the right of the shed, for example, is a real favourite: Stanier 8F 2-8-0 No. 48177, a very free steamer, which used to work the regular night train from the brickworks to London. In the shed are a couple of Midland Compound 4-4-0s (with their smoke-box doors open), and Standard class 5 No. 73003. In front, being prepared, is 2P 2-6-2T No. 41269, still fairly new, showing evidence of just having had its smoke-box cleaned, and to the left of the shed at the back is a Midland 1P 0-4-4T; such a familiar sight for so long on the push-pull services along Bedford's branch lines. Another 2-6-2T, No. 41270, is awaiting duties on the left, and at the bottom of the picture is the 0-6-0 class 3F locomotive No. 43222 with a tender full of coal, just raring to go.

Some 40 locomotives were based at Bedford in 1952, so, even allowing for those not visible inside the shed and those behind the camera, a lot of work was being performed on this day by the 15D allocation. (It was another six years before 15D was to become 14E.)

W. H. Allen's, one of Bedford's longest-established engineering works, dominates the area behind the shed and, judging by the steam and smoke pouring into the atmosphere, is equally busy but, for the moment, the main line running under Ford End Road Bridge (right/centre) is clear. Two or three coaches are being stored in a siding beside the Wellingborough bay of Midland Road Station, and these can be seen just above the bridge, yet the main sidings behind Bedford North Signal Box (gleaming white above the left-hand arch of the bridge) seem empty.

But for the shell of the shed and the main line, little remains from the bottom half of the picture, and much of the upper half is drastically altered. Allen's cooling towers are long gone, and a new office block replaces many of the older buildings. The new Midland Road Station was built more than 100 yards north of the old site, so the word 'Road' was quietly dropped from its title, and today it is just plain old 'Bedford'. The entrance is now half-way along Ashburnham Road, and not opposite the old Midland Hotel which, in recent years, itself suffered a name change, robbing it of its railway connotation.

Most of the photographs on the pages which follow also demonstrate the dramatic changes which have taken place on the county's railway system since the first line arrived in 1846, and one can only speculate on the changes which will occur during the *next* 150 years.

(P.E.B. Butler Collection)

2. (left) Bedford shed, about 1902. On the left is a Johnson 0-6-0 and centre, a 'Spinner', but the most interesting loco on shed this day is surely the one on the right, No. 2505, a Baldwin 2-6-0. In 1899 there had been an acute shortage of motive power on the Midland, the Great Northern and the Great Central so, because of a strike at certain domestic loco builders, all three companies decided to tackle the problem by ordering 2-6-0s from the USA; the Midland taking 30 (Nos. 2501 to 2530). They were used chiefly on coal and goods trains, but although they were fairly powerful machines, they suffered from a serious shortcoming – a very weak loco-brake! There were few fully-fitted non-passenger trains early this century, so it can well be imagined with what reluctance these unpopular imports were driven. By 1915 none was left, all having been replaced by Johnson and Deeley class 3 0-6-0s. The shed shear-legs (for lifting locos) are to the right of the roof, and W.H. Allen's cooling towers can be seen on the left.

(Bernard Matthews Collection)

3. (right) Sitting tender to tender, a pair of Johnson 0-6-0s occupy centre stage beside Bedford shed on Sunday 3 September 1933, showing two of the different styles of numbering and lettering in use by the LMS. No. 3329 is a class 3 locomotive; 3708 the smaller class 2. Introduced in the 1870s, dozens of similar 0-6-0s were shedded at Bedford over the years, and the last were not withdrawn until the 1960s. In this picture, the original ridge-and-furrow roof to the shed is very prominent, and can be compared with the flat BR version following the 1952 rebuild (see picture 1). Which do *you* prefer? *(H.C. Casserley)*

4. (right) Round about 1920. At the north end of Bedford's Midland Station, the lovely lines of the Johnson 4-4-0 main line express locomotive No. 314 are much in evidence as it backs down towards its train with safety valves lifting and a tender full of coal for the journey ahead. But why is Bedford being honoured by such a distinguished visitor? Built in June 1877 by Dübs of Glasgow, No. 314 was always a Skipton loco, so what was it doing so far south? Another mystery waiting to be solved. The loco lasted until November 1928, and isn't it a shame that none of this beautiful class was preserved? (*Bernard Matthews Collection*)

5. (left) Posing prettily, Neilson-built 2-4-0 No. 54 awaits its next turn of duty on a summer's afternoon in June 1922. Of 1870 construction and with the original number 821, it acquired a cab during rebuilding in 1888, and the number 54 as part of the 1907 renumbering. At Bedford it would have worked mostly on the branches, but would also have seen a certain amount of main line work on such jobs as piloting 'Spinners'. It is sad to report that sister loco No. 48 was one of the three locos written off as a result of the dreadful accident at Hawes Junction (Garsdale) on Christmas Eve 1910. Behind the coal wagon (right) is Bedford Junction signal box.

(*Bernard Matthews Collection*)

6. (left) On 15 September 1934 No. 115 (an ex-MR Kirtley/Johnson 2-4-0 of October 1874 with mixed frames) was coming off shed with a tender full of coal and a very smart crew, probably to take a train to Hitchin that Saturday afternoon. Since its introduction, the class had been seen all over the system but, at about 60 years of age, No. 115 was being allowed to see out its days on less demanding work along a nice quiet branch line. Built by Neilsons in Glasgow, the loco was originally numbered 78, was No. 115 in 1907 and became No. 20115 in 1935. The last 2-4-0 at Bedford, No. 20216, left in 1941. (R.G. Jarvis)

7. (right) Bedford Central signal box is something of a mystery as almost no information about it has survived, and this seems to be the only photograph of it. The location was immediately south of Ford End Road bridge, and it appears that the photographer was standing on the bridge to take the picture, although he was probably more interested in the locomotive than the box! The 2-6-0+0-6-2 Beyer Garratt No. 4998 was reportedly making the first ever visit by a member of this class to the town, and if true this dates the picture around 1927/8 when the loco was brand new. (P.E.B. Butler Collection)

8. (left) No. 3157 was one of the Johnson class 2 0-6-0s designed to supersede Kirtley's outside-framed class 1 locos of the same wheel arrangement, and was built in 1886. First used on coal and goods trains, it served a spell as a shunt engine at Kettering and later on trains between there and Huntingdon. As a Bedford loco it did regular runs on the Northampton and Hitchin branches, and looks all set to perform just such a duty on Saturday 22 June 1935 when this picture was taken. By 1947, 15D had only two of the class left (they were Nos. 3157 and 3164) but they were soon to be scrapped by British Railways.

(R.G. Jarvis)

9. (right) On 21 May 1963 there was a treat for local enthusiasts when the Holbeck-based Jubilee No. 45739 "Ulster" worked in from Leeds on a parcel train which terminated at Bedford. This was a regular turn for a Leeds Black Five or Jubilee of the period, and depended upon just what type of loco was available, but it had never been a common occurrence to see a '5X' on Bedford shed, so when one apppeared it was always an event to be savoured and treasured. Here, "Ulster" is on its way to the turntable, and after coaling and servicing will work back to its home depot some time later. (B. Wheeler)

10. (left) Stranger on shed. In February 1968 GER Holden 0-6-0 J17 No. 1217 was being towed from Hellifield to Brighton (to go in store at the Preston Park depot) when a hot box was detected near Bedford, and to avoid further damage, the loco was detached and put on shed. No stranger to Bedford, as No. 65567 (of March Depot) it was often to be seen on the St John's line, but never, so far as is known, had it been here on Bedford Shed before. After a couple of weeks, a repair had been effected and the J17 continued on its way. As the preservation movement grew, more locos were saved for posterity, and No. 1217 is one of them – not in working order yet, just cosmetically conserved. It was first sent to Bressingham in Norfolk, but later went to the National Railway Museum in York.   (*M.P. Burgoyne*)

11. (right) Coincidentally, a mishap similar to that above had taken place four years earlier when Maunsell N class 2-6-0 No. 31851 was on its way to King's of Norwich for scrap, and came to grief near St John's. The locomotive was abandoned here for a fortnight in April 1964, reposing on the site of the old LNWR engine shed. As with No. 1217, 31851's over-heated bearing was later repaired, and the 'southern stranger' continued its journey to Norfolk on 28 April.

(*Robin Waywell Collection*)

12. (above) and 13. (below) 0-4-4Ts were long-time favourites on Bedford's branches and, since their introduction in the 1870s, seem always to have been seen in the area. No. 58053 was built in Derby in 1889 as MR No. 1832, acquired 1340 in the 1907 renumbering scheme and the number shown here in June 1948 under BR. Waiting patiently in the Northampton bay at Bedford on Saturday 19 March 1949, the nicely kept 0-4-4T contrasts vividly with the run-down appearance of the once magnificent platform canopy at the north end of the station. By the early 1950s, the roof had been rebuilt in a flat and far less appealing style. Twelve years earlier the same photographer had been at Bedford shed to capture a similar (but different – note cab, side-tanks, bunker etc.) 0-4-4T as it sauntered about on its day's work. Equally smart, and sporting the 1936 block-style shaded lettering, No. 1230 had been built by the Avonside Engine Company (Bristol) in December 1877 and worked as No. 32 on the Somerset & Dorset Joint Railway for much of its early life, becoming their No. 52 in August 1928. The 1230 number was allocated in 1930, and it was kept until withdrawal. That, happily, was still a few years away on this Saturday in July 1937, the loco looking as if its bunker had just been replenished under the newly commissioned coaling tower, seen here partly hidden behind the ash plant on the left.

(Both pictures: H.C. Casserley)

14. Ten Crosti-boilered 2-10-0s were introduced as a modification to the very successful Standard class 9Fs in an attempt to effect some economy in coal consumption by pre-heating the water before it was fed into the boiler. The pre-heat boiler was situated immediately below the main boiler, and the exhaust was via a special chimney on the right-hand side of the locomotive. Despite the dull weather, these features are clearly visible on No. 92028 as it takes the avoiding line north through Bedford on Thursday 4 September 1958. Bedford Shed oversees the right-hand side of the picture, and below it a 3F 0-6-0 brews up behind the coach. To the right, in front is the ex-Lancashire & Yorkshire class 2P 2-4-2T No. 50646 which, because of operational difficulties, spent most of its time at Bedford in store, and just visible behind it is the Britannia Pacific No. 70042 "Lord Roberts", temporarily moved to this position after failing on main line duty some weeks earlier. The end of the Crosti-hauled train is just passing Bedford's most prominent feature, the coaling stage, which was to outlast the locomotive (in this form) by many years. Maintenance costs were so high and footplate crews so disliked the Crostis that it was not long before all had been converted to conventional draughting, although they were always easily recognisable as having been 'converts'.   (*Ken Fairey*)

15. (right) The cold winter of 1962-63 will long be remembered for its heavy snowfalls, and as usual Britain's railways suffered extensively with blockage after blockage. Being fairly flat and open, the lines around Bedford were subjected to much deep drifting of snow in the strong winds, so special steps had to be taken to keep routes open. Derby sent two snowplough-fitted 4Fs to Bedford (No. 43955 was the other), and between them they shared clearing duties on the lines which suffered most – the branches to Cambridge and Northampton. The Harpenden to Hemel Hempstead line was also cleared in this way, but there is no sign of snow on Bedford depot as No. 44214 takes a breather shortly before returning to its home depot. *(John Parker Collection)*

16. (left) Class leader. Very similar to the Stanier Black Fives, the BR Standard class 5 4-6-0s were introduced in 1951 and worked over most of the railway network. No. 73000 was on Bedford shed on 8 March 1957, receiving attention from a fitter, bravely ignoring the escape of steam under pressure from the first safety valve. Whilst the loco was coasting down from Sharnbrook summit for the stop at Bedford with a Leicester-St Pancras semi-fast passenger train, shortly before this picture was taken, a piece of scale had lodged in the safety valve, causing steam to escape uncontrollably. There was just enough left for No. 73000 to abandon its train in the station and limp on to shed for the scale to be removed before continuing its journey. Withdrawal of the class had started by 1964, but fortunately, five have found their way into the hands of various preservationists dotted around the country. The nearest one to Bedfordshire is No. 73050, named "City of Peterborough", based on the Nene Valley Railway at Wansford. *(F.G. Cockman)*

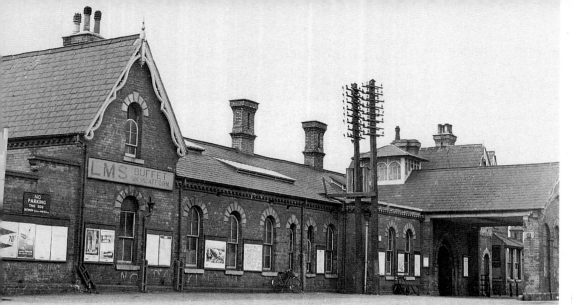

17. (left) and 18. (below) Bedford Midland Road Station will be remembered with varying emotions by thousands of RAF National Service personnel as the gateway to Cardington Camp, the place where they did their basic training. Opened in 1859, the exterior view (photographed circa 1948) shows the soon-to-be-removed LMS buffet sign, typical Midland bargeboards, the lantern house (to illuminate the booking hall) and the porte-cochère where intending passengers could alight from their vehicles in the dry on wet days. Passengers at Bedford were afforded every luxury! In the picture below (dated 1955) Esther is peeping out of her cubby-hole, waiting to collect tickets and being dwarfed by the stately dimensions. During demolition the GPO removed the post-box from the wall to save it from the sad fate that befell everything else depicted here. The replacement station was opened by Sir Peter Parker in 1978.

Left (*F.G. Cockman Collection*) Below (*F.G. Cockman*)

19. (left) Bedford Station as it was soon after opening on 1 February 1859. The photographer is standing under Ford End Road bridge looking towards Leicester, with what was then the Midland Main Line carrying on to Hitchin behind him. After the London extension had been opened to St Pancras in October 1868, and Midland Road Station considerably enlarged, the lines nearest the camera became the Hitchin bay. The centre of the picture is where the booking hall stood and the lines in the distance had various jobs, including use by some Northampton trains, eventually becoming known as 'The Dock' by local railwaymen. Bedford 'cut-off' lines were to go sweeping past on the left.

(*S. Summerson Collection*)

20. (below) When the new Midland Road Station was being built in 1978, Bedford North signal box was ever-so-slightly in the way, so a modern 'Portakabin'-type replacement was erected a few yards north of the original, and operations transferred there. When this, in turn, became redundant two years later, it was not destroyed on site as its more attractive predecessor had been, but was carefully dismantled and moved to Northampton for further use.

(*P.E.B. Butler*)

21. (above) and 22. (right) Sheer elegance. Bedford North signal box features prominently in these two pictures of 'Spinners' going south, and its appearance was not to alter much until it was demolished to make way for the new station in 1978 (see picture 20). The locos are early versions of Johnson's graceful 4-2-2s (with either 7 ft. 4 in. or 7 ft. 6 in. driving wheels) – the one in the top picture is on a through train and that on the right on a stopper – and they differ slightly from the later versions by having slide valves and smaller diameter driving wheels. In both pictures, Bedford's tall and elegant semaphore signals are being used artistically by these early railway photographers to balance the scene around the trains. Nearly 100 years later, today's cameramen still strive (often unsuccessfully) to achieve exactly the same effect.

Above (*J. Adams/National Railway Museum*)
Right (*G.W. Tripp/National Railway Museum*)

23. On Saturday 18 April 1936 there was an un-named Jubilee on Bedford Shed. No. 5649 had entered service in January of the previous year, and had run anonymously until being named "Hawkins" a couple of months after this photograph was taken. Interestingly, one of the nameplates is now resident in Bedford, part of a private collection. *(J.M. Jarvis)*

24. Standard class 4 No. 75056 prepares to leave platform 5 of Midland Road Station with a teatime train to Wellingborough, and Stanier 8F No. 48374 passes through platform 4 with a northbound express goods on Saturday 2 August 1958. To the right of the class 4 is the loco shed water tank (above Ford End Road bridge), and on the left is a reminder of gentler times when the usual way to work was by bicycle.

(*S. Summerson*)

25. This reverse view of the picture opposite shows the north end of Midland Road Station, always a popular place with both train-spotters and photographers alike (station staff permitting!) as it gave a good view of all the movements through and past the station with the single exception of trains on the Hitchin branch. After lunch, the light could be difficult for photographing the trains taking the avoiding line, but careful exposure would achieve acceptable results. On Monday 5 March 1956 Holbeck (Leeds)-based Jubilee No. 45639 "Raleigh" hurries through with a St Pancras-bound express, whilst 3P 2-6-2T No. 40165, Bedford's long-time carriage-shunt locomotive, sits beside Bedford North signal box, patiently awaiting work.

(J. Parker Collection)

26. An ex-Crosti-boilered 9F 2-10-0 eases southwards through Midland Road Station with a coal train on Saturday 23 May 1961. Although quite handsome locos, the 10 rebuilt Crostis did not have smoke deflectors (all the others did), and thus retained their 'different' look, even after being modified to conventional operation. That none of the original 1859 station was preserved is a crying shame. With typical ridge-and-furrow roofing (and attractive cast iron foliate brackets to support it), the station should surely have been carefully dismantled with a view to reconstruction, possibly at some Midland-orientated preservation centre such as Butterley. Instead, the complete structure was smashed to smithereens on site and carted away wholesale for scrap. Nobody at the time seemed to care that such an important piece of Bedford's history was being legally vandalised and totally destroyed.

(*R.J. White*)

27. Britannia Pacific "Arrow" takes the avoiding line. When Bedford cut-off was opened in 1894, the station was by-passed by the main line and stood, in effect, on the goods line. Trains not stopping here were therefore able to speed past round the back, as it were, which is what we see happening in this picture. No. 70017 runs between some standing vehicles in the station (left) and W.H. Allen's engineering works (just out of the picture, right) on Thursday 14 July 1960. The end of the train is just coming out from under Ford End Road bridge.

(R.J. White)

28. (above) and 29. (below) Portraits of perfection. So called because of their tendency to slip, the Midland 'Spinners' (built between 1887 and 1900) have quite accurately been described as Samuel Johnson's most beautiful creation, and as No. 673 is currently on display in its marvellous Midland Red livery at the National Railway Museum in York, this claim may easily be verified. At the head of an express train waiting to leave Bedford for London, No. 119 of March 1899 is having its coal moved forward by the fireman as steam escapes from both safety valve and emergency whistle. Up until 1904, many locos were fitted with a smaller 'secondary' whistle (fitted beside the main) which acted as an early version of the communication cord, the connection to which is visible hanging down beside the tender. No. 130 of April 1899, also one of the later version of 4-2-2s with 7 ft. 9 in. driving wheels and piston valves, is on a train in the Hitchin bay, showing off its lovely lines beneath the finialled MR telegraph poles above Ford End Road bridge.

(Both pictures: J. Adams/National Railway Museum)

30. (left) No. 18 rests under Ford End Road bridge in about 1900. These 0-4-4Ts were a particularly successful design, and were used all over the system having been introduced in 1875 by Johnson to supplement the sturdy Kirtley outside-framed locos of the same type. Here, they worked the Northampton and Hitchin branches, and from Wellingborough they ran to Higham Ferrers. They will be fondly remembered from before World War II days as the locos which replaced the old Webb 2-4-2Ts on the rail-motors between St John's and Bletchley, No. 1260 (see picture 187) being a particular favourite.

(G.W. Tripp/National Railway Museum)

31. (below) Built at Derby in 1880, No. 1481 was renumbered 231 in 1907 and withdrawn in 1929: a life of about 50 years which was by no means an unusual achievement for many Victorian locos. The scene is the Northampton bay at the north end of Bedford Station, and the date is round about 1902: the 2-4-0 having been shedded at Bedford from 1899 to 1905. It is interesting to note that the line to the shed (see picture 27) has not yet been installed. If it had been, it would occupy the space at the very bottom of the picture. *(G.W. Tripp/National Railway Museum)*

32. A beautifully posed picture of Bedford South with its signal box in Victorian times. Four tracks cross the River Great Ouse here, each pair on its separate bridge. The back bridge (largely hidden) is the original 1867 construction and, at the time of this photograph (1898), was being renewed, an exercise that was to be repeated some 80 years later at the time of electrification. The bridge nearer the camera was opened in 1894 as part of the avoiding line scheme and, perhaps surprisingly, remains largely unaltered more than 100 years later. The new Midland shed was rendered inaccessible when the avoiding lines were built, and its site was behind the trees to the left, the turntable being towards the river. The allotments (bottom) lasted well into the 1970s, but the general view is unrecognisable now, being dominated by mature trees, unruly undergrowth and an assortment of dowdy-looking boats at the water's edge. Known locally as Twin Bridges, this was long a popular viewpoint for Bedford's trainspotters, although it is doubtful if many dressed as well for the occasion as the gent on the left who, one would like to think, might well be enquiring of his friend behind the fence when the next 'Spinner' is likely to appear!

(*National Railway Museum*)

33. Royal Scot class 4-6-0 No. 46140 "The King's Royal Rifle Corps" comes off Bedford's Twin Bridges (see picture opposite) with an afternoon express for St Pancras in the summer of 1959. The train has just taken the avoiding line past Midland Road Station, and as the loco is sporting a 16A shed plate, the train could possibly have come from Bradford or Manchester. With the exception of the track, virtually all the railway features shown here have gone. The coaling stage (seen above the second coach), the gantry and other semaphores (at the end of the train and on the right-hand side of the picture), Bedford South signal box (right), all the telegraph poles, the fence and even the allotments with their wooden huts (left); none survives. The gas-holder (left-hand side) *is* still there, although the Bedford Gas Works (which was situated right beside the Bedford shed) went at the time of the universal changeover to natural gas. *(David Eatwell)*

34. Bedford's Midland Station at the turn of the century. Kirtley 2-4-0 No. 153A sits in the London platform with a mixed rake of coaches forming a stopping train to St Pancras whilst one of the crew enjoys the late afternoon sunshine as he leans nonchalantly against his charge awaiting the off. The white circle on the down platform home signal (above the second coach) dates the scene as pre-1909, as it was during 1908 that the circle became the stripe we all recognise today. No. 153A had been rebuilt with a different boiler in 1900, was renumbered 20 in 1907 and was withdrawn in 1921. Fortunately for us, a similar locomotive, No. 158A of 1866, is preserved in immaculate external condition at the Midland Railway Centre, Butterley.

(G.W. Tripp/National Railway Museum)

35. At the end of the 1950s, when this picture was taken, 'The Waverley' was one of only a few 'named' trains on the Midland main line out of St Pancras. As its name implies, it went to Edinburgh, but in all honesty, the Midland can hardly have expected many passengers who wanted to go there from London to spend about 10 hours on *their* train, when they could have made the journey from the adjacent terminus (Kings Cross) in half the time! Leaving the capital at about 9 a.m., the first stop was Nottingham, and the train went via Leeds City (where there was an engine change and a reversal) and Carlisle (where there was another engine change). Of course, going over both the Settle & Carlisle and the Waverley route on the same train must have attracted more than a few sightseeing travellers, but surely, only those with a day to spare would have gone the whole hog. The loco, No. 45532, is the rebuilt Patriot "Illustrious", and here it is bursting out from under the old Kempston Road bridge which was replaced and raised at the time of electrification in the early 1980s, although the abutments may still be seen from passing trains. In the background is one of the brand new Rolls Royce diesel multiple units just leaving for St Pancras.

(*David Eatwell*)

36. About a mile south of Millbrook signal box, an unclassified road crosses the railway near Millbrook village, and is the only public bridge over the 10 mile stretch of line between Bedford and Flitwick. In consequence, the location was well used by locals both for train-spotting and for photography, as Millbrook up home starter semaphores vied with lineside telegraph poles for prominence in the wide open spaces of the Vale of Bedfordshire. On Monday 4 December 1961, Stanier 8F 2-8-0 No. 48377 is about to pass under the bridge with a London-bound coal train, coping well with the strong winter wind and the almost continuous 1 in 200 up grade from Bedford to Leagrave.   (*F.G. Cockman*)

37. (left) During World War II, Wilstead Ordnance Factory (the cause of much speculation by local lads as to its use at the time) had an extensive railway system, and the entrance to the depot was controlled by this interesting little signal box. Coming into use on Sunday 3 August 1941, it stayed open for a surprisingly long time after the war, not closing until Sunday 8 September 1968. A small platform within the confines of the site was brought into operation at the same time as the signal box for use by workers from both the Bedford and Luton directions, but by May 1946 it had been closed. Today, some lengths of rail may still be seen set in concrete around the place, but as trains speed past unhindered on the Midland Main Line, most of their occupants are probably unaware of the contribution to the war effort made by what has now been renamed, rather ignominiously, Elstow Storage Depot. The story goes that the name Wilshampstead was shortened by the Eastern National bus company because it was too long to fit in the space on the front of their buses. Whatever the reason, the village is now universally known as Wilstead. *(P.E.B. Butler)*

38. (right) Millbrook signal box was one of those remote and isolated boxes, miles from anywhere, with access either by rail or via a bumpy dirt track across the fields. A sort of 'lowland' version of the box at Ais Gill, Millbrook stood proud on a bit of an embankment about half way between the Coronation Brick Works at Chimney Corner and Ampthill Tunnel, and although its very remoteness contributed much to its attraction, it suffered from the inconvenience of not being connected to mains water. Even as late as 1977 when this official photograph was taken, water was still being delivered by rail when required. No trace of its existence remains now, although the track across the fields still sees use by PW gangs working on the electrified Midland Main Line. Opened in October 1893, the box was raised to improve visibility in 1913, but finally succumbed on 1 June 1980.

(Harpenden Railway Museum Collection)

39. (above) and 40. (opposite) Spot the differences! These two pictures of Midland Compounds emerging on the fast line from the south end of Ampthill Tunnel were taken about 45 years apart, and haven't things changed in the meantime? The original 1868 line through here was only double track, utilising what was later to become the slow tunnel, the one shown in these pictures on the right. When the line was quadrupled in 1895, it looks as if the Midland Railway employed someone with the talent of Capability Brown (above) to landscape the area, as hardly a single blade of grass seems out of place. The left-hand (fast line) tunnel mouth is recognisably the same in both pictures, and above it can be seen the drainage channels crossed by the diagonal footpath, but about the only other similarity is the stone-built retaining wall beside the slow line. The picture above is dated about 1905 when the Compound would have been brand new, and the picture opposite, with LMS still on the loco's tender, was taken between November 1948 when 41017 was re-numbered, and August 1950 when it was withdrawn.

(Above: *Andrew Underwood Collection*. Opposite: *L.N. Owen/John Parker Collection*)

41. A hundred yards south of Ampthill Tunnel, the wide cutting is spanned by an extremely elegant six-arched bridge which has been well used over the years by photographers both as a vantage point (the photograph opposite was taken from it) and as a frame for trains passing under it (the picture above and picture 246 show this aspect of it to some advantage). The cost of construction of such a substantial overpass must have been totally out of all proportion to its use, as at no time did it ever really lead anywhere! Never more than just an occupation bridge, it is boarded off and has no use whatsoever today, in consequence being extremely difficult to access from above, should the inclination to investigate it ever crop up. Sometime in the early fifties, Black Five No. 44918 storms through on an afternoon Nottingham-St Pancras express, well demonstrating the affection with which this particular 4-6-0 was held because of its brilliant steaming and free-running capabilities.

(Peter Chapman/Andrew Underwood Collection)

42. No. 70054 "Dornoch Firth", one of the few Britannia Pacifics with a coal-pusher in the tender, emerges from the 'new' fast line tunnel at Ampthill on the up 'Thames-Clyde Express' one summer's evening in 1959. On the right, an unidentified 9F breaks out into the daylight with a goods train, the crew no doubt gulping in large amounts of fresh air at the end of their ordeal in the confined spaces of the original 716-yard 1868 bore. When it was constructed, no air vents were thought necessary, so the lack of consideration by the Victorian engineers was cursed by footplatemen thereafter as they coughed and wheezed their way up the 1 in 200 incline through the fume-filled orifice as quickly as they could. The 1895 tunnel-builders learned their lesson, though, as these later excavations of the 2-yard-longer tunnel provided wider clearances and proper ventilation for the fast-line trains.

(*David Eatwell*)

43. There is an old story about the residents of Dent complaining to the Midland Railway when the Settle & Carlisle Railway was being built, that the station bearing the name of their community was too far away. 'Sorry, we can't do anything about it,' said the authorities at the time, 'but the station has to be on the railway.'! You can see what they meant, of course, but it wasn't much help, and a similar conversation may well have taken place when the site of Ampthill Station was being discussed in the 1860s. Initially much busier than Flitwick, its relative inaccessibility played no small part in its eventual demise in 1959. There was only one member of staff (a booking clerk) employed at Ampthill during the last two years of the station's existence, but this scene shows a fairly high degree of over-manning with both a porter and a junior porter on duty as a seven-coach stopping train gets away from the up main platform one winter's day in the early 1950s. A shift-change seems imminent in Ampthill signal box, too, as what looks like the figure of the relief signalman is plodding up the platform with his bicycle to take over in the box (see picture 45), visible at the south end beside the departing train's locomotive.

(Andrew Underwood Collection)

44. What a way to spend the war! Sid Beale was Ampthill's long-time porter, and in fact only left the station when staff were no longer required because of lack of custom in the late 1950s. This garden on the down main platform was Sid's pride and joy, and certainly brightened up the otherwise drab appearance of a small country station in wartime. To the left can be seen the back end of Bobby's Bus, well known to all users of the station at the time as the main conveyance between there and the town centre. The platforms were oil lit, the result of the reluctance of the local Gas Company to run its pipes to the station, but after the war the Electricity Board felt no such reluctance, and Ampthill ended its days electrically lit (see picture 45).

(*Andrew Underwood Collection*)

45. Ampthill signal box, just off the south end of the island platforms, was unusual in that it had a pair of skylight windows set in the roof on the north side (well illustrated in this early '50s photograph). But why should the windows be there at all? It seems that the up home signal at the end of the platform was so close to the box that the signalman couldn't see from the side window if the lamp was lit, hence the installation in the ceiling. Standard class 5 4-6-0 No. 73049, no more than a couple of years old at the time this picture was taken, comes in with a stopping train for Bedford, passing between the coal yard behind the box (left) and the parcels bay (right).

(Peter Chapman/Andrew Underwood Collection)

46. External facilities! Backing on to the High Street, yet mainly hidden from that busy through route, Flitwick signal box stood a few yards north of the platforms, and was set into the side of the cutting on the up side of the line. The first box here was in use by 1875, and one is left to wonder what toilet arrangements the earlier signalmen had to suffer before the introduction of the luxury lavatory provided by BR as shown in this late picture. The box itself bears a striking resemblance to many on the Midland (see picture 38), but none of the others seem to have been able to match the splendid amenities afforded to the fortunate few at Flitwick. Less lucky lever-pullers had to perform in the confines of the more usual wooden lean-to. This view is dated May 1978, just two years before final closure. (*P.E.B. Butler*)

47. (opposite) and 48. (above) Like so many stations on the Midland, Harlington had much appeal to travellers and trainspotters alike, being very conveniently placed in the village, able to provide good vantage points to view the passing trains. On Wednesday 6 June 1939 one of our most renowned railway photographers honoured the station with his presence, capturing (as well as the picture opposite) this nostalgic view of the scene in 'the good old days' before the last war. At that time LMS Jubilee No. 5654 "Hood" was a Derby loco, and on this gloriously sunny afternoon it was rostered to haul the 12.25 express from Manchester to St Pancras, due through here some four hours into its journey. Twenty years later, "Hood" had become a Millhouses loco, and remained a regular performer on the Midland Main Line. Earlier the same afternoon (opposite) Harlington had witnessed the passage of No. 757, one of Johnson's classic class 3 4-4-0s, heading north on the 14.40 train from St Pancras to Kettering. Introduced in 1900, the last members of the class survived until 1952, but sadly none was preserved. On the left, class 4F 0-6-0 No. 3967 lazes about by the goods shed on pick-up duty, and Harlington Station's best-known feature, the signal box, stands out prominently on the down fast platform. Saved from destruction at the last moment, the typical Midland box was painstakingly dismantled, and is now to be seen again in working order, following careful reassembly at the Buckinghamshire Railway Centre, Quainton Road, near Aylesbury.

(Both pictures: H.C. Casserley)

49. (opposite) and 50. (above) Two-and-a-half miles from Luton, Leagrave marks the culmination of 17 miles of almost continuous upgrade south from Bedford. Mainly at 1 in 200 but with a few short sections of light relief, the line drops gently from here to Luton, so that when travelling in the opposite direction firemen knew that by Leagrave they would be able to take things a bit easy until they crossed the River Great Ouse just before Bedford Midland Road. The smooth exhaust from these two northbound 4-6-0s implies a certain amount of inactivity on the respective footplates as little physical effort would be needed for the next quarter-of-an-hour or so. In the picture opposite, Stanier Jubilee 4-6-0 No. 45609 "Gilbert and Ellice Islands" seems the epitome of health on Monday 19 May 1952 as it heads a down express between the original Midland Railway goods-shed (left) and Leagrave signal box, giving no indication that it would be the first of the class to go when the withdrawal programme began a few years later. (No. 45637 "Windward Islands" was actually the first Jubilee taken out of service, but that wasn't so much withdrawn as written-off – a result of the awful accident at Harrow in the same year this picture was taken.) Above, we get a powerful view of the Appleby milk empties, seen on Monday 19 October 1955 travelling north behind Black Five No. 44943. The diagonal shadows on the platform are cast by the attractive Midland lattice fencing seen for so long adorning many stations up and down the main line, but now mostly swept away by modernisation.

(Both pictures: Harold Clements)

51. For nearly 90 years, Leagrave Station had only two platforms, but in readiness for the introduction of the forthcoming diesel multiple units which were due to start in January 1960, it was decided in the late '50s to construct the hitherto missing slow platforms, and at the same time to modernise the whole station, including rebuilding the footbridge with clearances suitable for any future electrification scheme. Somewhat surprisingly, the original station building (with coal fire in the booking hall/waiting room) by the down fast platform was left more or less unaltered, and even today boasts something of a rarity in its outside wall – an Edward VII post-box by the main entrance. On Friday 7 November 1959, Riddles Standard 9F 2-10-0 No. 92050 trundles through the new platform with an up van train, passing a young schoolboy signalling for the train to stop. He doesn't really believe that he will succeed, does he – or does he? (S. Summerson)

52. Rarely photographed and used only 'as required', Limbury Road signal box controlled a 1918-built coal yard on the up side of the line about a mile south of Leagrave. Established during WWI to relieve congestion at the Crescent Road yard, Limbury was used by local coal merchants until it became the aggregate store it is today. Speeding past on a down express is the preserved Jubilee class 4-6-0 locomotive No. 45690 "Leander", a rare visitor indeed to the Midland Main Line. Probably borrowed to fill a last minute motive power shortage on Sunday 15 June 1958, "Leander" was shedded at Bristol Barrow Road, causing its appearances in this part of the world to be very few and far between. Two Jubilees from 82E found their way to the Barry scrap yard in South Wales, but whereas "Leander" has been beautifully restored to main line running order, the other, No. 45699 "Galatea", remains a rusting hulk at the time of writing, and seems unlikely ever to receive such tender loving care. But you never know ....

(S. Summerson)

53. (opposite) and 54. (above) As late as June 1962 when these two pictures were taken, the view from Luton's Roman Road bridge was much as it had been for many years previously. The wide open spaces looking north towards Leagrave Station (left) and the broad shallow cutting with the houses in Marsh Road backing on to the railway looking south (right) were very inviting to photographers; these two pictures showing off the Midland Main Line north of Luton Midland Road Station to good advantage. The passenger train (opposite) is an up Bradford express hauled by Jubilee class 4-6-0 No. 45562 "Alberta", and the goods train (above) consists of coal empties from Brent with the rebuilt Crosti 9F No. 92024 having just passed Leagrave's up starter semaphores. The brake van is about to pass under the four-arch Waller Avenue bridge, but how different these settings are today with the electrification poles and wires dominating the scene, and the linesides comprehensively overgrown. Waller Avenue bridge itself has now been completely rebuilt, its shapely arches giving way to a flat-topped concrete construction, gaining sufficient clearance for the wires, but losing the appeal the old brick-built structure had presented since its erection. The neat allotments (left-hand side of picture) have long since gone, and Marsh Road's houses are now virtually invisible behind a great depth of mature trees and bushy shrubs. The open spaciousness of the '60s is sadly missing from the present day constrictions so apparent to any observer of current railway operations.

(Both pictures: S. Summerson)

55. With a good load of coal still evident in its tender, BR Standard 9F 2-10-0 No. 92109 from Wellingborough, wheels a long train of household coal past the North End goods shed at the approach to Luton Midland Road Station on Monday 21 April 1959. This coal train is undoubtedly destined for the large marshalling yards at Cricklewood, north London, and, showing prominently on the left, track revision has started prior to the anticipated introduction of the new Rolls Royce diesel multiple units on the Bedford to St Pancras suburban service.

(*S. Summerson*)

56. Midland Railway 3F 0-6-0 No. 43665 ambles through Luton Midland Road Station on the up side with a short train of well-loaded 16-ton mineral wagons on Tuesday 21 April 1959. The 3F is vacuum fitted, but it is doubtful if this facility was often taken advantage of in the latter days of its active life. A member of a class of 575 locos introduced in 1888 by Samuel Johnson, No. 43665 was rebuilt under Henry Fowler, who gave it this large boiler and Belpaire firebox.

(*S. Summerson*)

57. (left) A pre-1923 Midland Railway angle of the western side of Luton Station reveals a timeless scene in bright summer sunshine. The poster board is headed proudly MIDLAND RAILWAY, telegraph poles stand resolutely and evenly-spaced along the station length, the humblest of railway servants brush-and-shovels up the horse droppings (for the station gardens perhaps?), and a new-fangled motor car, totally open, contrasts dramatically with the miscellany of horse-drawn carts. Ah, happy days. (*Bernard Matthews Collection*)

58. (right) 2P 4-4-0 No. 40550 and Jubilee class 4-6-0 No. 45607 "Fiji" come to a halt at the up main platform in Luton Midland Road Station on Wednesday 8 April 1959 to pick up a good load of passengers bound for St Pancras. With diesels soon to appear on the Midland Main Line, express trains were accelerated in advance of the new equipment being delivered, thus pilot loco-motives were reverted to at this time to maintain the tight schedules. The end of a northbound passenger train is just visible pulling away from the down platform, whilst over on the up goods line a heavy load of coal is heading south towards the metropolis. (*S. Summerson*)

London to Manchester "Midland" Express, passing Luton at full speed

59. (left) Issued in the summer of 1907, this old postcard shows a northbound express train storming through Luton Station en-route from St Pancras to Manchester Central. On the up platform city businessmen await their rail transport to London, which will probably be close behind the light locomotive seen disappearing on to the right-hand curve to the south. On the down platform a plethora of porters stand by for unloading and loading duties when the next stopping train arrives.

(*Harpenden Railway Museum Collection*)

60. (below) Looking southwards from the down main platform at Luton's Midland Station, an enormous number of staff pose for this undated 'official' photograph. Note particularly the canopies, as well as the old advertisements, the main line tracks and the ancient apparel of the platform posers. (*Bernard Matthews Collection*)

61. Surprisingly still sporting the 1950s 'Lion and Wheel' emblem on its tender, Royal Scot 4-6-0 No. 46122 "Royal Ulster Rifleman" pulls away from Luton Midland Road with an express for St Pancras on Saturday 11 March 1961. In the foreground the signal wires from Luton South signal box trail along parallel with the down main, and the first class passenger in E15284 (right behind the tender) should be engrossed in his book for at least another 35 minutes.

(*S. Summerson*)

62. On Tuesday 27 June 1961, 4MT 2-6-4T No. 42686 of Bedford was caught passing through Luton Midland Road Station, moving smartly away from Crescent Road Yard, south of Luton, on the slow line with a well-loaded rake of hopper wagons attached to the down local pick-up goods. In this view the revised track layout can clearly be seen, with the down slow platform line diverging from the through line, whilst the up and down main lines to the right of the picture remain as they always were.

(S. Summerson)

63. As late as 1956, the all-conquering combustion engine was not quite so all-conquering in railway goods delivery services as might have been imagined. Photographed in Luton's Guildford Street (not far from the town's railway stations) in April of that year, no less than eight years had passed since nationalisation, yet the flat cart still proclaims LNER and LMS along its edge, although the faithful horse has sadly succumbed to the modern era by having a BR blanket wrapped around its hindquarters! It is a nice sunny day, and no doubt the driver is quenching his thirst in the hostelry behind the ensemble – let's hope he brought a pint out to satisfy the motive power's thirst and didn't get nicked for being drunk in charge of a horse!

(S. Summerson)

Park Square, Luton

59478. (JV)

64. Luton's experience with tram cars was a relatively short-lived affair, lasting just 24 years. Opened in 1908, there were five routes, between them linking the town centre with Dunstable Road, Wardown Park, Round Green and Ashton Road, whilst horsebuses were used to serve those areas not covered by the trams. However, in 1932, this still young standard-gauge system was abandoned in favour of the fast developing motor bus. Looking towards Park Square in the early 1920s, we see Tramcar No. 10 clattering along the single track section, away from the square, travelling in the direction of the Ashton Road terminus. It is not possible to say whether the small boy between the cyclist and the tramcar is trying to cross the road or patiently waiting for No. 10 to stop for him, but as the top is completely empty there is plenty of room for him to enjoy the view during the journey, should he wish to en-tram. The boy on the left seems to be in full flight to get home, whilst the little dog on the right is definitely escaping for its daily constitutional. To get to Luton's railway stations, you will have to turn right down Church Street at the road junction behind the tramcar, between what is now the Arndale Centre and Luton University, totally unrecognisable today from the view in this fine old locally-published postcard.   (*Wardown Museum*)

65. Working hard, ex-Crosti-boilered 9F 2-10-0 No. 92025 heads northwards through Luton's Midland Road Station using the slow line on Saturday 27 May 1961. Note the covered wagons under the canopy of the goods shed on the left, and the usual grotty condition of the 9F. If one of these had ever been cleaned during normal service the world might well have lost a generation of trainspotters, all dying from shock at the sight!

(*L. King*)

66. Just three days after Christmas, 8F 2-8-0 No. 48261 is passing Luton Midland Road Station in fine style on the down slow line on a very wintry, snowy Friday in 1962. The load in tow is the daily Cricklewood Yard to Sundon rubbish train, and one can almost feel those tarpaulins over the wagons flapping and fluttering as the train speeds past the camera, swirling up the loose snow in its wake. The large warehouse and loading/unloading sheds behind the wagons on the left were a distinctive feature at the south end of Luton Station, but were swept into oblivion as needs changed in the mid-1960s.

(S. Summerson)

67. A fascinating angle of Luton's two stations, looking north on Wednesday 2 March 1949, showing a little bit of Crescent Road Yard on the right, and the Midland main running lines on the left. Further back are the old LNER tracks into Bute Street Station, and an 0-6-2T N2 is facing downhill towards Welwyn and Hatfield. To the left of the N2 is the long closed Church Street coal yard, and at this time in 1949 there was no physical connection whatsoever between the ex-LMS tracks and the ex-LNER tracks; the two great companies never acknowledging each other's existence in Luton! (No explanation is offered as to why the van is blocking the crossing on the right … could it just have been forgotten?) It was only the complete closure of the Luton to Hatfield branch in 1965 which compelled the engineers to install a trailing connection (by January 1966) between the Midland down fast line and the remnants of the ex-LNER branch to Dunstable, which survived just for traffic to the Blue Circle Cement Depot in Houghton Regis, the Total Oil Depot in Tavistock Street, Dunstable, and one or two other local industrial sites.

(*M. Burgoyne Collection*)

68. 8F 2-8-0 No. 48414 poses for Commer's official photographer alongside Crescent Road yard on Tuesday 22 March 1949, before heading away northbound with a load of boxed Commer components from the local Luton factory. These had been loaded one large box per wagon, and in all probability would be tarpaulined over after the photographer had finished. Note that 15 months had passed since the railways had been nationalised, yet there is still no number plate on the front, and the letters LMS are still on the tender. Another 8F waits on the right, and in typical 1949 manner, No. 48414 has been carefully positioned with rods down, although no thought seems to have been given to small details, as surely no 'official' photograph should have been taken with a telegraph pole sticking out of the loco's dome.

(*M. Burgoyne Collection*)

69. Accelerating away from Luton on the up main line, LMS 3-cylinder compound 4-4-0 No. 41048 passes the 29-mile post and heads south on the 13.37 semi-fast train from Bedford to St Pancras on Friday 26 August 1955. The ever-expanding Vauxhall car manufacturing plant can be seen dominating the eastern side of the tracks in this interesting study, just at it does (but even more so) today. (*Harold Clements*)

70. Climbing the last few hundred yards at 1 in 200 away from Luton on Thursday 14 October 1954, the summit will soon be reached for the driver of Beyer Garratt 2-6-0+0-6-2 No. 47982 on a long haul of coal from Nottinghamshire, all destined for the fire grates of millions of Londoners, well before the general advent of central heating and clean air! The first three trucks in the train are ex-private-owner wagons, and the fourth is a brand new 16-ton mineral wagon of BR design. Once over the summit, No. 47982 will drop at 1 in 176 through Chiltern Green and cross the border into Hertfordshire. Luton's southern ring road now goes over the line exactly at this point.   (*Harold Clements*)

71. (left) An outside-framed Midland Railway 0-6-0 No. 2788 heads an up slow goods train at East Hyde, south of Chiltern Green Station, on Thursday 18 September 1924. Although it is only a year after the Grouping, the fourth wagon proudly carries LMS along its side planking, whilst the others still bear allegiance to the erstwhile Midland Railway. The class 1 Goods 0-6-0 was designed by Matthew Kirtley, the Midland Railway's first loco superintendent, in 1868, and in 1943 there were still 11 of this class in active service.

(*Harpenden Railway Museum Collection*)

72. (above) Approaching Chiltern Green Station on the down slow line, Beyer Garratt 2-6-0+0-6-2 No. 47972 is working a wonderful variety of empty wagons from Brent Sidings (Cricklewood) to Toton in Nottinghamshire on Saturday 10 March 1956. This particular loco had cost £10,002 to build in 1930, covered 588,101 miles, and after a lifespan of a little over 26 years it was finally despatched to the big engine-shed in the sky on 6 March 1957. The only folk sorry for the demise at the time, apparently, were the enthusiasts who had admired and cherished this fine-looking but misconceived class during the three previous decades. None was preserved, but if one had been, wouldn't present day enthusiasts have relished the task of putting it back in order?

(*Harold Clements*)

73. (right) A glistening Midland Railway Belpaire 4-4-0 pulls to a halt at the down main platform at Harpenden Station during the early years of the twentieth century. A few passengers await the semi-fast service, whilst over on the down slow platform a suburban train pauses, probably about to return to London. A fine array of enamelled advertisements shout their messages to passing Edwardian commuters from the Midland Railway fencing, and over on the up platform the usual heap of wicker baskets await forward transit. (*Harpenden Railway Museum Collection*)

74. (above) The elegance of Midland Railway operations is typified in this circa 1895 angle of Harpenden Station. Two spotlessly clean Midland Railway locomotives head southwards with an express train, a host of wicker baskets await transport later in the day, and in these Victorian times, the up side goods shed presents a really busy scene with a host of wagons to be dealt with. Handsome lamp standards parade along the length of both platforms, and a gaggle of spectators admire the two locomotives heading for the St Pancras terminus, speedily to be reached in half-an-hour or so.
(*Harpenden Railway Museum Collection*)

75. Oakley Junction, still in all its glory in August 1952, with Jubilee No. 45615 "Malay States" of Kentish Town coasting through on an up express, having clearly had a successful top-up on Oakley water troughs a few minutes earlier. The loco, its exhaust-steam-injector leaving a trail behind it, carries one of the few Jubilee boilers to remain domeless, and the train, interestingly, is composed of ER stock. The Northampton branch disappears behind the row of parked wagons to the left, but today, nothing of this attractive scene remains except the four through running lines. Opened to traffic on 10 June 1872, the only access to the junction was from the southerly (Bedford) direction, but this was no real inconvenience as trains from further north could reach Northampton direct from Wellingborough. The official closing date of Oakley Junction was 20 January 1964.

(*Geoff Goslin*)

76. On Wednesday 17 August 1977, the official photographer visited Sharnbrook signal box (still gas lit) probably to illustrate the layout of the new junctions as shown on the track diagram above the levers. The 'signalman's' name is not recorded, but as he is not recognised by local experts, he may well have been recruited for his photographic appeal! His careful choice of soft-soled footwear would undoubtedly have endeared him to the regular men, as not a scratch on the shiny lino is likely to have resulted from this very professional pose. There were signal boxes at Sharnbrook for 112 years ... the original was opened in 1869, was replaced twice during the next 20 years or so, and closure finally occurred on 17 May 1981. (*BR/Harpenden Railway Museum Collection*)

77. (above) and 78. (opposite) Oakley Troughs, situated about a mile north of Oakley station, came into use on 5 February 1904 and were the first in operation on the Midland Railway. Located by MP54, they considerably speeded up the timetable for expresses by cutting out the otherwise unnecessary stops at Bedford or Luton and, by encouraging the careful overfilling of the tender, the authorities cut down on carriage-cleaning costs as well! In the picture above, the fireman of Kentish Town-based Royal Scot class 4-6-0 No. 46162 "Queen's Westminster Rifleman" is enthusiastically operating the 'train-wash' mechanism as he speeds north past the lone figure of the lampman (left), but in the picture opposite such a ruse is hardly necessary as it is pouring with rain. Here, Leeds Holbeck-shedded Caprotti Black Five No. 44753 heads a fully-fitted down express goods train over the troughs in the early 1960s, almost at the end of their life. Most through trains were diesel-hauled by then, and after more than 60 years of wetting the heads of many an unsuspecting passenger, Oakley water troughs were finally decommissioned on 5 October 1964.

(*David Eatwell*)

79. Crewe-built (but Horwich designed) 2-6-0 No. 42904 works well on a down fully-fitted express goods train as it hurries past Souldrop signal box on Thursday 21 April 1960. Nicknamed 'Crabs', 245 of the class were built between 1926 and 1932; withdrawal getting under way in 1962. By 1967 they were all gone, except No. 2700 which is at the National Railway Museum in York, and Nos. 2765 and 2859 which are privately owned. The signal box closed at the end of 1966. The train is soon to breast Sharnbrook Summit, scorning use of the less steep goods line (behind the box) running through the tunnel.

(Ken Fairey)

80. Crosti 9F No. 92022 is here on the gentler-graded goods line nearing Sharnbrook Tunnel with a northbound train on Saturday 16 August 1958. The fast and slow lines are separating just here to allow trains like this to avoid the 1 in 119 climb to Sharnbrook Summit, but passenger trains would not normally receive such 'kid-glove' treatment and would speed over the steeper slope almost unhindered. Today, the goods line *is* still in use, but only just! It has been singled between Sharnbrook and Harrowden Junction (north of Wellingborough) in recent years, and we must hope that the current 50% reduction in size does not soon become 100%.   (*S. Summerson*)

81. (above) and 82. (opposite) Two pictures on the Nene Viaduct, Wellingborough; both taken on Christmas Eve 1959. The above photograph shows Black Five No. 44667 on a relief express train, and in the view opposite, 9F No. 92124 passes with an up slow goods. It is here that the fast and slow lines' gradients change, the latter using the much easier (but slightly longer) route through Sharnbrook Tunnel compared with the 1 in 120 climb to Sharnbrook Summit taken by trains on the fast line. The urgency being shown by both locos is probably not unconnected with thoughts of roast turkey and Christmas pud.

(Both pictures: Peter Groom)

83. The station at Little Irchester was known as London Road, and was about a mile south of Wellingborough. So called because it was the first station to connect the town with London, it was on the Peterborough branch of the LNWR (formerly the London & Birmingham Railway). To reach the capital, passengers would travel through Northampton to join the main line at Blisworth, and there change on to a Euston train. A bit roundabout, perhaps, but at the time (pre-MR), people were only too pleased to have a connection, and after all it was little different from Bedfordians having to go to London via Bletchley. Photographed from high up the nearby grain silo, this rural scene has much to commend it, so of course it couldn't last! Totally swept away, the site is now crossed by the A45 dual-carriageway road which actually uses some of the old track-bed. What price progress? *(Bernard Matthews Collection)*

84. Still standing proudly overlooking the railway today, the Morris Motors water tank had been a part of the 'fixtures and fittings' around Wellingborough since Thomas Butlin's Foundry occupied the site long before Morris took over. Making castings and engine blocks for the motor industry, the factory was one of the town's major employers, but today the whole area is an industrial estate with no railway connection. The locomotive, No. 61381, is one of Thompson's successful B1 class 4-6-0s which were introduced in 1942. Variously known as 'Springboks' (after the name of the class leader), or 'Antelopes' (after the names applied to 40 members of the class) there were more than 400 of them in service when construction ceased in 1950. No. 1264 has been preserved, as has No. 61306, now carrying the name "Mayflower". *(Ken Fairey)*

85. Trains for Northampton used the southern end of Wellingborough Station, and latterly were worked by Standard class 2 tank engines fitted for push-pull working. On a wet Saturday 2 August 1960, 2-6-2T No. 84008 had a little over five years of life left, while the Northampton line had less than four. It is somewhat ironic that the last 10 of this class existed for only eight years – built 1957, scrapped 1965. What a waste!

(R.J. White)

86. A very smart Midland Compound, No. 41198 of Leicester, returns to home base at the head of the 15.20 semi-fast from St Pancras, leaving Wellingborough one sunny evening in 1957. On the left, the Higham Ferrers local waits to leave, behind a class 2 2-6-2T, but neither train seems to have proved very attractive to the travelling public, judging by the pronounced inactivity on the platforms. (*John Harrison*)

87. What's this, coal going *north* through Wellingborough? Yes indeed, and all the indications are that it is slack-coal for Stewarts & Lloyds, Corby, having come up from Bargoed in South Wales. A 4F and a Black Five occupy two of the roads in the carriage sidings on Saturday 15 April 1961, and the overall scene with 8F No. 48386 about to pass under Mill Road bridge can only remind us what a wonderful place Wellingborough was for watching trains. Note the classic Midland double-slip points on the left (beside the 'abandoned' van) for example, and the general impression that scenes like this would last forever. But of course they couldn't, and of course they didn't.   (*L. King*)

88. Nottingham-based 46118 Royal Scot class "Royal Welch Fusilier" catches the low afternoon light on Boxing Day 1960, taking a Manchester express from St Pancras away from Wellingborough after the short stop. On a sweeping curve, the station was a particularly photogenic location with its attractive buildings, semaphores and the pièce de résistance, the station signal box dominating the north end of the platforms. On this Monday after Christmas, not too many people would want to be travelling, one supposes, but the usual nine-coach train would have to run, just in case.

(*Peter Groom*)

89. A B1 on Wellingborough shed, and a 3F 0-6-0T, but how different from No. 47279 (see picture opposite). An MR locomotive, No. 47211 (being transferred to Gorton), had been a London loco (hence the tell-tale condensing pipe) and is one of the class first introduced in 1899, 25 years earlier than the LMS-built version. The B1, No. 61051, would have worked in from Sheffield during the week and, after simmering idly here for a while, would have taken a train back there later. Sundays were always good days for shed visits, and this one, 5 August 1962, was no exception, even though it was getting on towards the end of steam. The exact location is behind Wellingborough North signal box (right), the building on the left doubling as the wheel-drop and the steam-crane shed. On the subject of the 3F, don't let any local railwaymen ever hear you call it a 'Jinty'! In this part of the world, only to trainspotters were the 3F 0-6-0Ts called 'Jintys'; to the professionals they were 'Jockos'.

(Ken Fairey)

90. Sunday afternoon in Wellingborough No. 1 roundhouse. Five locos of four different classes (left to right: 8F, 9F, 8F, 4F and 3F) await next week's activities on 10 February 1957. No. 47279 (on the right) will hold special memories for people in the area for, although it was a Bedford loco for a short period, it spent most of its life shedded at Wellingborough. Even today, it is still held in much affection by aficianados of preserved railways, as it can be seen in all its restored glory on the Keighley & Worth Valley Railway in Yorkshire.

(*Ken Fairey*)

91. Wellingborough North signal box is featured in this picture, along with some 9Fs taking a Saturday break on shed in 1957. The two nearest the camera, although both Wellingborough 2-10-0s, are very different. Poking out from behind the box is No. 92054, a conventional 9F, whilst No. 92028 is one of the 10 Crosti versions of the original design. At this time wearing a single deflector, it was, like the other nine, soon running around with the Crosti equipment out of use and partly removed, rendering these modified locomotives much better liked by drivers and firemen as a result. The pointed roofs above the signal box were on No. 1 Shed; the round tank was part of the water-softening system; the two-road shed behind the locomotives housed the breakdown crane on one road, and there was a wheel-drop on the other. The brick building on the right had been the repair shop, and further to the right (out of the picture) was No. 2 Shed which has lately found a new lease of life with Whitworth Foods.

(*John Harrison*)

92. With the somewhat ecclesiastical appearance of Wellingborough's No. 1 roundhouse beside it, class 4F 0-6-0 No. 44263 gets well away with an up goods train on a dreadfully dull day in 1957. Trailing the standard LMS-design of tender, No. 44263 was a member of the largest class of locos in the country at the time building ceased in 1941. After a construction period which spanned 17 years, there were eventually 772 4Fs, although this total was to be well beaten by the 842 Black Fives built by the LMS and BR up to 1951. Even this figure was beaten, but only just, by Collett's GWR 0-6-0PTs – this *was* the record-holding class with 863 locos. *(John Harrison)*

93. 0-6-0T 'Jocko' No. 47273 is seen in this view looking north from Finedon Road bridge as it trundles across the main running lines with a couple of box-vans and a Midland brake on Saturday 15 April 1961. The Wellingborough Iron Company's sidings curve round to the left, and the whole scene reminds us how important Wellingborough and its railways were in the days of steam. The Iron Company's employees will remember the brick building on the left with feeling – it was the pay office – and enthusiasts will remember Neilson's Sidings (in the distance); Finedon Road (here) and, behind the photographer, the sheds and the station where there always seemed to be much activity with continuing movements, both major (through expresses) and minor ('Jockos' shunting) to enjoy.

(L. King)

94. Ex-MR 0-6-0 class 3F No. 43624 shunts iron-ore wagons in Wellingborough's Tipperary Sidings on Saturday 3 March 1957. On the right, the old Midland provender store stands proudly overseeing the comings and goings, and in the centre, the Wellingborough Iron Company's works are just visible through the murk. The air may very well be cleaner these days, but 1957 clearly wins hands-down for atmosphere.

(*L. King*)

95. Running for about five miles from Wellingborough, the Higham Ferrers branch was built – reluctantly, it seems – by the Midland Railway as a result of pressure by local boot and shoe manufacturers who wanted a more convenient railhead (for the despatch of their products) than that provided by the (then) nearest stations: Irchester or Irthlingborough. Initially only goods trains used the line, the first one reaching Higham in September 1893, but because of the necessity to build extra platforms at Wellingborough, a passenger service did not start until the following summer. There was only one intermediate station, that at Rushden, now home of the Rushden Historical Transport Society, and along with its goods shed it is almost the only remaining feature of the whole enterprise. A single line from Irchester Junction, the branch sometimes hosted locos the size of a class 4, a class 5 or even a Jubilee, but more often than not motive power consisted of small tank engines, typical of which is the ex-Somerset & Dorset 0-4-4T No. 1230, shown above waiting to leave Wellingborough for Higham with a bunker full of coal on Saturday 4 November 1933. Fitted with Ramsbottom safety valves, No. 1230 was a class 1P, introduced on the Somerset & Dorset Joint Railway in 1877, and had a non-standard Belpaire boiler which it was to keep all its long life until withdrawal in 1946. They don't build 'em like *that* any more!

(*J.M. Jarvis*)

96. Not quite a sister to No. 1230 (see picture 95) but definitely a close relative, MR Johnson 1P 0-4-4T No. 58091 (LMS No. 1430) awaits the off at Wellingborough on Thursday 19 April 1951 with the 09.10 motor-train to Higham Ferrers. With somewhat increased tractive effort, the 205 members of this very similar Midland class were introduced in 1875, the locomotive shown here being the last one built, in 1900. The Higham platforms were on the east (up) side of the station, the branch trains using the Midland Main Line slow (goods) tracks between Wellingborough and Irchester Junction.

(*H.C. Casserley*)

97. The construction of extra platforms at Wellingborough caused a delay of nine months after the first goods trains ran before passenger services could start along the branch in 1894, but it was not for a further 35 years or more before any Fowler 3P 2-6-2Ts were seen at Higham Ferrers. Introduced by the LMS in 1930, there were 70 of these 3Ps, and Wellingborough (15A) had one or two for a time, although they only appeared here for short periods. Passenger trains on the branch were known variously as 'The Rushden Gusher' or 'The Higham Flyer', depending probably upon where the speaker lived, but whether they 'gushed' or 'flew', their progress could never honestly be described as anything other than sedate. Speedy they weren't! Soon to leave for Higham, No. 40061 (above) was photographed at Wellingborough around 1957/58.

(John Harrison)

98. Rushden Station in June 1993, showing the beautiful condition in which the Rushden Historical Transport Society has maintained it. Various vehicles, including steam locomotives, have been on show here, and the well-stocked bar is rightly renowned for its welcoming atmosphere. An unusual locomotive which spent some time at Rushden was the traction-engine lookalike, an Aveling & Porter 0-4-0WT, now restored to working order, and sometimes to be seen chuffing round its present home at Hunsbury Hill, Northampton, with happy passengers in tow. In this picture, the locomotive is an Andrew Barclay 0-4-0ST, Works No. 2323 of 1952, which came here after being crawled over by countless children of all ages whilst it was part of the attractions at Wicksteed Park in nearby Kettering. Before Wicksteed, No. 2323 was employed at S. Durham Steel & Iron Co. Ltd quarries in Irchester, and went to Cohen's of Kettering for scrap in 1969. It was rescued from Cohen's, was at Irchester Recreation Ground for a while, and the rest, as they say, is history; although restoration to working order, if at all, is very many years away.

(P.E.B. Butler)

99. Nicely framed by the occupation over-bridge, Standard class 2 motor-fitted 2-6-2T No. 84006 sits at Higham Ferrers on the far end of its train, waiting to propel it back to Wellingborough on Thursday 28 May 1959, just two weeks prior to the withdrawal of passenger services from the branch. These came to an end on Saturday 13 June, the last train being hauled by sister loco No. 84007, specially smartened up for the occasion. The goods service lingered on for another $10^1/_2$ years to November 1969, but soon after that the whole area was cleared and, although the building saw some further use, it eventually had to go. Today, visitors would never guess that there had ever been a railway here, the new houses occupying the site not really having the character of the lovely old Higham Ferrers Station.   (*Ken Fairey*)

100. End of the line. When the original Act authorising the Higham branch from Wellingborough went through Parliament, the intention was for the line to continue to Raunds and a junction with the Kettering-Huntingdon line, but for some reason (never satisfactorily explained) it only got as far as this point. Here, looking northwards off the station bridge on Saturday 29 June 1955, we see the full extent of the branch past the station in the direction the line would have taken had it gone on to Raunds. The loco is a Fowler 4F 0-6-0 No. 43861, and it is simmering away in Higham goods yard, getting ready to leave with a short working to Wellingborough. The goods shed, stone-built and substantial, has been completely demolished and the site cleared, but what happened to the 'rubble'? Such stone blocks would surely have had some further usefulness, and could quite possibly have been re-used in a local building project. Some of the houses standing where Higham Station once stood are stone faced. Perhaps …?

(H.C. Casserley)

102. Higham Ferrers terminus. Taken just into the peace after the horrors of World War II, the really rural setting of Higham Ferrers is well illustrated in this view from the station bridge, showing the 16.15 motor-train setting off for Wellingborough in lovely low late afternoon sunshine. The date is Friday 10 August 1945, and the train is just starting its five mile journey, the booked time for which is about 12 minutes, including the stop at Rushden. No. 1246, a Johnson 1P 0-4-4T of a class dating from 1875, had larger driving wheels than the 1881 class, and lower tractive effort (see picture 12), but was visually very similar. No. 1246 was withdrawn in 1949, still with its LMS number, but by 1954 the remaining locos of this charming little class had all been done away with, not one being saved for preservation.　(H.C. Casserley)

101. (opposite) Awaiting return to Wellingborough. Passenger services on the branch still had three years life left when this scene of typical hustle and bustle (!) was captured at Higham Ferrers on Saturday 28 July 1956. The shadows tell that the time of day is late into the afternoon, and the invisible locomotive is the LMS 2P 2-6-2T No. 41277, waiting to take its two-coach push and pull train back to Wellingborough, the driver comfortably seated in his cab at the front of the train, whilst his fireman takes care of all the heavy work on the footplate of the locomotive at the back. The Midland Railway's influence is evident, not least by the lattice fencing on the left, and the delicately finialled gas lamps bear witness to the thoughtful imagination of designers from times long gone by. Fortunately for us, many of today's preserved railways are recreating scenes like this, although their survival, too, depends on them attracting a few more passengers than this to their terminus stations.
　　(L. King)

BEDFORD TO HITCHIN

104. In the same bay as the picture opposite, but at the other platform, 3F 0-6-0 No. 43474 awaits departure with a parcels train for Hitchin in July 1959, blissfully ignoring the state of things to come in the shape of one of the unpopular Park Royal-built diesel railbuses sitting alongside. Not only did these 'new-fangled' machines prove to be mechanically unreliable, they also suffered from an unfortunate tendency to derail on facing crossovers when taken at any speed other than a walking pace, so their dislike by drivers is hardly to be wondered at. Transferring them to Scotland did much to help staff/management relations at 14E at the time! When Bedford station was first opened, this pair of tracks formed part of the main line from Leicester (see picture 19), but became the Hitchin bay when the London extension opened in 1868. The shadow at the bottom is of Ford End Road bridge, seen so prominently in the previous picture. *(R.J. White)*

103. (opposite) The Bedford to Hitchin branch was once a main line! Right from its conception the Midland Railway was desperate to reach London, and when the 16¼ mile long double track line was formally opened on 7 May 1857, Midland trains worked as far as Hitchin where their passengers changed on to the Great Northern Railway. Later, the Midland exercised running rights through to King's Cross, but, not unnaturally, the GN signalmen at Hitchin always gave precedence to their own trains, sometimes causing M25-type tailbacks along the line from Bedford. Accordingly, the partnership was never a happy one, so the Midland Railway was obliged eventually to strike a new line southwards through Luton and St Albans to the grand new terminus at St Pancras, which opened in 1868. Thus the Bedford to Hitchin line rapidly deteriorated into a typical branch line, and remained so until closure early in 1962. Eventually singled over most of its length, motive power on the branch provided more variety than most. A staple diet of ex-LMS 2-6-2Ts was the norm for the last 12 years of its existence, but a sensation occurred amongst the loco-spotting fraternity in March 1956 when ex-Lancashire & Yorkshire Aspinall-designed class 2P 2-4-2T No. 50646 was transferred from Royston in Yorkshire to Bedford for the purpose of working trains along the branch. Unfamiliarity meant that the new arrival, so far from home, was little used and, indeed, this occasion on the afternoon of Saturday 28 July 1956 is thought to be the only time No. 50646 successfully worked to Hitchin and back. Here, the exile is awaiting departure from the bay at the south end of Bedford Midland Road Station, and we must wonder if the lad at the carriage window has any idea of the significance of the event. *(L. King)*

105. A scene of prosperity at Bedford goods depot as the shunter takes a few moments off from a hectic morning of coupling and uncoupling wagons to admire Ivatt 2-6-2T No. 41271 drifting past Ouse Bridge signal box and heading with its one coach load for the Hitchin branch. Beyond Ford End Road bridge in the background lies Bedford Midland Road Station, and the main lines curve away beyond the gaggle of huts and sheds behind the signal box. A class 3F 0-6-0T 'Jocko' can be seen simmering behind the box van in the depot yard, and will no doubt soon be busy again once the Ivatt 2-6-2T has cleared the section on its way to Hitchin. The date is Saturday 3 June 1961.

(Peter Waylett)

106. Crossing the River Great Ouse in Bedford on Saturday 23 April 1960 is Midland Railway 3F 0-6-0 No. 43428, heading for Midland Road Station with just a one-coach load. But what a pristine and gleaming 'load' it is! Only a few days out of Wolverton Carriage Works following a complete overhaul and repainting, the coach has been trip-worked over from Bletchley to Bedford St John's, and the station pilot at Midland Road has been sent down to St John's to work it back on to the Midland Main Line, for it soon to resume revenue-earning service. Photographed from the same footbridge as No. 41271 opposite, Kempston Road bridge is shown in the background, and the area behind the 3F is the site of the new Magistrates Courts. No. 43428, a stalwart of Bedford loco shed, arrived on depot from Wellingborough in the early 1920s, and stayed until withdrawal in December 1962.

(S. Summerson)

107. Activity on, and very recently under, the Ouse bridge. The date is Saturday 28 May 1988 and the time 07.45. The rowing four are practising for the annual regatta on the River Great Ouse, and Brel Ewert's Standard class 4MT 2-6-4T No. 80080 has travelled south from its base on the Midland Railway Trust at Butterley in Derbyshire to take part in an exhibition in the goods yard, immediately south of Bedford Midland Road Station, in connection with the two-day River Festival over the weekend. This bridge, the first railway crossing of the Great Ouse in the town, carried the erstwhile Hitchin line and the spur round to St John's Station, but by the time this picture was taken, track alterations had resulted in the abandonment of all routes other than direct access on to the Bletchley line. The later bridge carrying the Bedford-St Pancras main line can just be seen amidst all the trees in the distance. *(David Eatwell)*

108. Midland Railway 0-6-0 class 3F No. 43428 is halted at a home signal with a northbound goods train on the double-track section at Southill Station on Friday 16 November 1962, nearly a year after the branch line from Bedford to Hitchin has closed to passenger services. A couple of covered wagons are still stabled in the loading bay on the southbound side, and it can be seen that while the Hitchin-bound passengers were afforded the luxury of covered accommodation in which to shelter from inclement weather, those bound for Bedford were treated very frugally indeed. But the local 'Lord of the Manor', owner of nearby Southill Park, never had cause to worry about such mundane matters as shelters – he was in the unique position of having the right to stop any train he chose, although contemporary records don't seem to show how frequently, if at all, he actually exercised his option. The station building is now a splendid private residence, and well worth a lingering glance should you be passing – by road, of course! (Ken Fairey)

109. (left) and 110. (below) Two Midland Main Line stations – Southill (left) and Cardington (below). Both, happily, still survive. Photographed in 1965, the substantial nature of the MR's building is well shown here, as is the similarity of the architecture. Southill is slightly larger than Cardington, but neither station was anything like adjacent to the community it purported to serve. For 10 years in the 1850s and 60s, MR expresses from Derby and the north would nip along here on their way to Hitchin for London, and passengers were unavoidably presented with these views of impressive wayside stations, probably built more for show than for usefulness. That they are still here today can be no greater tribute to the MR and the men who built them.

(*Both pictures: Bill Wharton*)

111. (above) Henlow Station in the early 1930s. A Midland Railway 3F 0-6-0 shunts in the yard, and will ultimately be on its way along the line through Shefford and Southill, and then to Bedford. Fine Midland Railway architecture epitomises the fact that, for virtually a decade in the mid-nineteenth century, this had been the Midland Railway's main artery from the industrial Midlands to London. In 1939 the left-hand platform was extended to cope with larger trains, and the track slewed across, rendering the platform by the building redundant (see picture114).   (*Bernard Matthews Collection*)

112. (right) Classic detail of the Midland Railway is shown in this view from the Hitchin-bound platform at Henlow Station. The all wood constructed signal box is typically Midland, as too is the wooden post signal which is situated exactly where the old northbound track once lay. A huge water tank rises above the signal box roof, undoubtedly the self-sufficiency supply of fresh water to the RAF camp nearby. Note the signalman's personal motive power parked at the foot of the steps – one bicycle!   (*P.E.B. Butler Collection*)

113. Bright springtime sunshine throws a well defined shadow on to the embankment as 3F 0-6-0 No. 43333 lifts its safety valves on the downhill stretch of track at Ireland (between Southill and Shefford) on Saturday 5 March 1960. Withdrawn in 1961, this locomotive was one of three of the class to be fitted with 6 ft. driving wheels in 1906 specifically for working important time-sensitive fish traffic in the north of England. No. 43333 reverted back to the standard 5 ft. 3 in. wheels in May 1924, and survived another 37 years in service with the LMS and British Railways. When the line from Hitchin to Bedford was singled, this section was deliberately retained as double track to afford a passing loop on the $16^{1}/_{4}$ mile long route. The hamlet of Ireland consists of nothing more than a very attractive row of cottages and a pub called 'The Black Horse', but surely 'The Shamrock' or 'The Leprechaun' would have been a more appropriate name for the only inn in Ireland in England!

(*S. Summerson*)

114. Ex-Great Eastern Railway class J15 0-6-0 No. 65479 (of a 289-strong class) looks its age as it waits at Henlow Camp on Saturday 28 May 1960 for the RAF personnel to emerge and head for the capital on a 36-hour leave pass. This platform at Henlow had been lengthened in December 1939 to accommodate large wartime troop trains, yet the 'temporary' nature of its wooden construction was somewhat belied by the fact that it was still going strong, more than 20 years later. No. 65479 was allocated to Hitchin MPD specifically for leave train duty, having replaced E4 2-4-0 locomotive No. 62785 as the branch engine a couple of years previously, and this train, formed of two of Gresley's infamous 'sit-up-and-beg' quad-art sets, ran every Saturday morning from Henlow Camp to London. The train was unadvertised from Henlow to Hitchin, where it changed locomotives and continued on as the 11.43 Saturdays Only working to Broad Street. The service was discontinued at the end of the summer timetable in 1960 as Henlow Camp's car parks became increasingly busy, and the J15 was withdrawn for scrap that August. The building to the right of the loading-gauge is 'The Bird in Hand' pub, still a popular meeting place for airmen and women, but an industrial estate occupies the site of Henlow Station, no trace of which can be seen today.

(*S. Summerson*)

115. The passenger trains have been discontinued, but a goods service still lingers as 3F 0-6-0 No. 43521 is shown a clear signal through Shefford Station, allowing it to head towards Henlow and Hitchin on Friday 16 November 1962. The goods yard, visible beyond the road under-bridge, still seems fairly well used, and new concrete-sleepered track in the foreground might well be a gentle piece of costly investment produced at the right moment to justify complete closure of the line, thus proved to be totally uneconomic! *(Ken Fairey)*

116. (left) The precarious nature of Shefford Station's high position is well shown in this ground level view, revealing the all-wooden construction and the huge angled joists holding the whole structure in place. A covered stairway led up to the platforms, and a sloping path gave access to the other end of the building. Now all the remnants of the railway are long gone and the site has been totally redeveloped, but there is a reminder of times past in some nearby street names, and the nostalgically named pub – 'The Bridge'.

(Tom Rounthwaite)

117. (right) Midland Railway Kirtley-designed 800 class 2-4-0 No. 61 comes to a halt in Shefford Station en route from Hitchin to Bedford, quite obviously on a windy day as the passengers prepare to join the train. Locomotive No. 61 was built in December 1870 as Midland Railway No. 828, was renumbered No. 61 in November 1907, survived the First World War and was withdrawn for scrapping in April 1922, just eight months prior to the demise of the Midland Railway and the formation of the LMS.

(Bernard Matthews Collection)

118. Viewed from the down platform at Hitchin on Tuesday 30 October 1962, 3F 0-6-0 No. 43453 makes its way off the Bedford Branch and crosses all four of the East Coast Main Line tracks in order to access the up platform, from which it will then propel its wagons into the yard just north of the station on the east side of the main line. Behind the guard's brake van can be seen Cambridge Junction signal box, and above the middle of the train is the signal gantry controlling traffic coming in from Royston and Cambridge. Even today, conflicting movements occur as northbound suburban trains traverse all four main running lines at this point on their way to Cambridge, but few regret the dismantling of the old gas works, seen to the right behind the locomotive.   (*S. Summerson*)

119. Its work done in the up side goods yard, 3F 0-6-0 No. 43453 regains the up slow line over some wonderfully complicated pointwork and runs into Hitchin's up platform on the same date as the picture opposite. From here it will continue beyond the station and go on shed for perhaps some servicing and certainly turning before heading back along the branch to Bedford. The impressive buildings on the down side of the main line were the Great Northern's goods sheds, somewhat overshadowing the nearby Midland's efforts at what was once their southern extremity. Their thrust towards London in this direction was only short lived as they soon dispensed with running rights over Great Northern metals to King's Cross and opened their own route from Bedford through Luton into the magnificent terminus at St Pancras – just a stone's throw from their rival's terminus. The Midland may have been dwarfed by the GN at Hitchin, but they made quite sure the same thing didn't happen in London.

(S. Summerson)

120. (above) While the traditional wheel-tapper makes his way along the photographer's train, all movement on the LNER's East Coast Main Line has come to a stop as LMS 2-4-0 No. 226 has brought its four ancient coaches from Bedford right across all the running lines into the up platform at Hitchin Station sometime before 1932. Once all the passengers are detrained, No. 226 will withdraw to the ex-Midland premises for turning and servicing, then pick up its four coaches again, and return along the branch line to Bedford from the down platform. The roof and vents from Hitchin's LNER MPD show up prominently above the platform wall, and note the enamelled advertisements on the right, similar to those which can be seen at most preservation railway centres today.   (*John Parker Collection*)

121. (right) A sabre-rattling cast iron warning notice still in situ outside the old Midland Railway property in Hitchin in 1975. It is difficult to imagine how any railway servant was able to determine whether a person upon the railway was actually on bona fide business or was indeed trespassing. Whatever, the sum of £10 was a lot of money by any standards, and one has to wonder if anyone was ever prosecuted successfully under the said Act. Note the unfortunate American influence in the fourth line – we in this country having been brought up to spell the first word 'licence'!   (*S. Summerson*)

122. It's Thursday 30 August 1962 and 3F 0-6-0 No. 43428 waits by the up platform in Hitchin Station for the signal, to gain access to the series of crossovers which will take it over all four Eastern Region tracks and back on to the sanctuary of the branch line to Bedford. Not many wagons have originated at Hitchin, but by the time it has shunted the yards at Shefford, Southill and, perhaps, Henlow, No. 43428 might well have quite a load on as it climbs towards Old Warden tunnel and drops down into Bedford, where it will deposit its train in the goods yard before retiring on to the Depot for a good night's rest.

(S. Summerson)

THE EAST COAST MAIN LINE
HITCHIN TO ST NEOTS

123. To have called the King's Cross to Edinburgh route the East Coast Main Line seems somewhat inappropriate since nowhere south of Newcastle-on-Tyne does the line get anywhere near the coast, and only achieves the distinction of doing so for a few miles either side of Berwick-on-Tweed, and for an equally short distance south of Dunbar in Lothian! But what's in a name? We all know (more or less) where the ECML runs, and the part which affects us here is the 20-mile stretch between Hitchin and St Neots, since most of that is in Bedfordshire. The first public train ran on the Great Northern between London and Peterborough in August 1850. This was not from King's Cross because of delays in the construction of the London tunnels and the terminus building, but a couple of years later all was ready and the official opening took place on 14 October 1851. The study of railway buildings is a subject on its own, most companies having adopted individual styles, and here is an interesting early photograph of the western exterior of Hitchin Station in Great Northern Railway days. The huge circulating area in front of it is now the car park, but here horse transport still rules and two drays await the arrival of the next train.

(Bernard Matthews Collection)

124. (left) One of the earliest railway photographs, this was taken in Hitchin Station during the very first years of the Great Northern Railway – circa 1855-59. Looking south it depicts 'Small Hawthorn' 2-2-2 No. 53 in original form standing tender-first in the up platform. Typical of the period are the low platforms, the curved footbridge and the almost total disregard the staff of the time seem to have had for oncoming trains. Either the locomotives of that era were too slow to be worth worrying about, or the chance to have one's visage etched for posterity on 'one of them new-fangled photographic things' was considered worth a dice with death. *(Bernard Matthews Collection)*

125. (above) The splendid, taller than average, Hitchin Yard signal box, stands sentinel over the passage of a traditionally grimy Riddles 9F 2-10-0 No. 92147 on an up goods on Saturday 25 March 1961. The train, composed mainly of steel-bodied 16-ton coal and mineral wagons, interspersed with a handful of the wooden-bodied 'five-plank' variety, is passing a magnificent array of ex-GN signal gantries. With the exception of the goods shed, this scene has now been swept away in favour of the modern electrified railway. *(L. King)*

126. (opposite) Hitchin locomotive yard was a cramped, elongated affair, sandwiched between the station and a steep cutting hewn out of local chalk by the builders of the Great Northern Railway. Recessed against the face of the cliff and often tantalisingly out of sight to platform-based spotters (because of the presence of stabled locos on the nearer shed roads), there was a 60 ft. vacuum-powered turntable, installed to replace a damaged one in December 1949. On Tuesday 7 June 1960 it was being used to turn what at that time was the shed's one and only J15 0-6-0, No. 65479. A member of a ubiquitous ex-Great Eastern Railway class (and incidentally the last of the 289 J15s to be built, in September 1913), No. 65479 was shedded at Hitchin for working RAF leave trains to and from nearby Henlow Camp on the ex-Midland line to Bedford (see picture 114). When this picture was taken it had just two more months to live before withdrawal and scrapping at Doncaster Works. One classmate survives – No. 65462 on the North Norfolk Railway.   (*R.J. White*)

127. (above) This view illustrates well the 'party wall' nature of Hitchin shed – an ideal spot for young enthusiasts who could hang over the low wall and get as close to the locos as possible. It also shows the largely timbered nature of the shed roof and smoke vents – a constant fire risk. Taken 10 years into the tenure of the LNER, on Monday 5 June 1933, the picture shows D3 class 4-4-0 No. 4073 waiting to work south with a stopping train. The handsome, high-stepping D3s had their origins in the earlier D4 class, designed by Henry Ivatt in 1896, and No. 4073 was one of those rebuilt with a larger boiler between 1912 and 1928. (Locomotive modifications always seemed to be spread over much longer periods in those more relaxed times than is the case today.) Hitchin had two D3s at the Grouping in 1923, but by 1930 one had gone, leaving the other to share suburban slow train services with four classmates and the larger D2 class, all from King's Cross shed. Occasionally they would appear on main line expresses piloting Atlantics, but by the end of 1935 they had disappeared altogether from the southern end of the East Coast Main Line. It seemed as though that was the end, but the Second World War gave the class a new lease of life – so much so, in fact, that they were nicknamed 'Spitfires' by some depots – and Hitchin regained one in 1939. The class was extinct by the end of 1951.   (*Les Hanson*)

128. Storming through the centre roads at Hitchin on 2 March 1963 is Standard 9F 2-10-0 No. 92040, running fast-line with a partially fitted coal train, and clearly responding to the crew's frantic attempts to keep to schedule on this typically busy Saturday. No. 92040 was at the time allocated to the large locomotive depot at New England, Peterborough, and would most certainly be working its train through to Ferme Park sidings in north London. The rear of the engine shed is to the right of the picture, even providing a window through which waiting passengers might peer into the murky depths of this 'hallowed place'. Although Hitchin depot (coded 34D in BR days) mainly provided for secondary and local motive power needs at this important junction of the Bedford and Cambridge lines with the ECML, it did occasionally play host to top-line traction before closure to steam in June 1961, particularly the unique W1 4-6-4 streamlined loco No. 60700, which did not enjoy a very happy life and could often be seen receiving attention from Hitchin's fitters. The steam shed was subsequently demolished (although by default its two party walls remain) and its roster was taken over by a purpose-built diesel depot which had opened in the former Midland goods yard, at the north end of the station, in 1960. This, too, has now closed and is today used by Infrastructure Services for the maintenance of on-track machinery.

(S. Summerson)

129. With the chime whistle blowing, A4 Pacific No. 60013 "Dominion of New Zealand" is hurrying an up class C parcels train through Hitchin Station during the mid-morning of Sunday 24 April 1960. The photographer is standing on the up platform looking north, and what fine detail there is to be seen on both the magnificent signal gantry and the signal box immediately north of the down platform. Built in June 1937, No. 60013 avoided the preservation movement, finishing its working life at King's Cross Top Shed in April 1963, and being cut up for scrap soon afterwards. Note the complexity of the three-way point at the end of the platform alongside the A4 – a necessity dictated by the importance of having maximum standing room for trains in the platform and for having as long a siding space as possible in the goods yard.

(Ken Fairey)

130. Cadwell signal box sat right on the Hertfordshire-Bedfordshire border, controlling the gates for a narrow lane which meandered its way from Ickleford village to the western outskirts of Letchworth, and which crossed the East Coast Main Line a couple of miles north of Hitchin Station. On Sunday 27 September 1953, V2 2-6-2, still LNER No. 4821, speeds a fine selection of Gresley coaches northwards on the down main, while spectators, waiting to cross, stand by the gates on the east side of the line. This loco eventually became No. 60850 under the BR 1948 scheme, and had the ignominy of being in the first batch of three V2s withdrawn and scrapped in February 1962. In this view, the Cadwell signalman has been very quick in returning the 'peg', for all four of the signals partially hidden in the V2's smoke are at danger, with only the fifth coach of the train under the gantry.

(Harold Clements)

131. In common with some other stations on the East Coast Main Line, Arlesey was a notorious bottleneck, as there were four tracks either side of it, but only two tracks through it. Sandy, a few miles north, was just the same (see picture 137), and one must wonder with what affection (!!) drivers on the slow line held the route through Bedfordshire as a result. This 1959 view was taken from the signal box, and shows A3 Pacific No. 60063 "Isinglass", already with double-chimney, but still two years away from having its appearance totally transformed by the addition of 'elephant's ears' smoke deflectors. The train is on the up main, and has almost reached the level-crossing which was as popular with vehicle drivers on the A507 road as the lack of slow lines was with train drivers on the railway. Now there is an over-bridge, and four lines run through here, as they do at Sandy. Arlesey's new station was opened by Chris Green in October 1988, and the coal yard in this picture is the site of today's well-used car park.

(*David Eatwell*)

132. A wealth of past detail is on show in this evocative study of a northbound train trundling through Sandy Station yard in LNER days. The engine is No. 153, one of the trusty and powerful K3 class of 2-6-0s; this one eventually becoming BR No. 61845. These 'Large Moguls' were first introduced by Nigel Gresley in 1920, and their most striking visible feature was the height and diameter of their boilers in comparison with their overall size. Indeed, when they were first built, their 6 ft. boilers were the largest on the entire national railway system, and paved the way for the Pacifics of 1922. Gresley was so pleased with the K3s that he maintained production for 17 years, eventually turning out 193 examples. They were nicknamed 'Jazzers'. The type of train seen here is typical of a K3 payload – fast fitted or partially fitted vans numbering anything up to 50 vehicles. In the yard can be seen a cattle wagon, seven-plank dropside wagons (including several built up to contain livestock), ventilated vans, signals of all shapes and sizes, enamel signs, loading gauges, trackside huts, gas lamps, complicated crossovers; in fact, the lot. And what's left of all this today? Absolutely nothing!　　*(Soole Collection/National Railway Museum)*

133. (left) Enamel totem – or 'sausage' – signs from the 1950s and early '60s are now much sought-after items of railwayana, often fetching several hundred pounds apiece at auction. This particular one is known as a half-flanged type, meaning that the flange at the back extends only along the top and bottom ridges of the central section. It was also a remarkably late survivor, being photographed at night in August 1977 – some years after similar station signs had regularly begun to be 'half inched' by unscrupulous 'collectors'.   (*P.E.B. Butler*)

134. (below) Many enthusiasts feel that the Gresley A3 Pacifics were at their best, particularly from an aesthetic point of view, when fitted with double chimneys and German-style smoke deflectors, but the author is definitely not among them! This scruffy example of the breed, No. 60050 "Persimmon", is seen coasting nonchalantly northwards past the attractive and well-clipped topiary of Sandy Station on Thursday 28 March 1963, with an extraordinarily mixed bag of rolling stock forming either a parcels or empty coaching stock working. (The headlamp code indicates that it could be a parcels, newspaper, fish, meat, fruit, milk, horse, cattle or perishable goods train, composed of vacuum-braked stock. Such a rich variety and, except for parcels, all now lost to the railway.) And, immediately behind the tender, the highly incongruous sight of what appears to be a venerable six-wheeled former passenger coach.   (*Ken Fairey*)

135. A3 4-6-2 No. 60112 "St Simon" (last in the class) wheels an up express around the curve towards Sandy Station on a bright, sunny Saturday afternoon during the summer of 1957. The mix of rolling stock – Gresley, Thompson and BR – indicates a relief train, and this is confirmed by the special WTT (Working Timetable) number partially hidden by the vacuum pipe above the loco's buffer beam. To the right of this picture is the ex-LNWR line climbing away from Sandy Station, and it will cross the East Coast Main Line over the bridge just visible above the last coach of the train. The A3's tender has a healthy load of coal to see it over the final 44¼ miles to King's Cross, and this very smart Pacific still carries an excellent example of the early BR 'Lion and Wheel' totem, fondly known amongst the pundits as the 'Ferret and Dartboard'.

(*John Harrison*)

136. The driver of A3 4-6-2 No. 2746 "Fairway" has the regulator well open as he speeds a northbound express through Sandy on Saturday 25 May 1935. However, the old three-axle rigid-wheelbase GN baggage van at the front of the train must be inhibiting his speed potential on this run, and he will do well to maintain schedule. This A3 became No. 92 in the LNER's 1946 renumbering, and No. 60092 under BR from 1948. Built at Doncaster in December 1928, "Fairway" spent most of its working life shedded at one or other of the two Newcastle area Motive Power Depots, and indeed was withdrawn from Gateshead shed in October 1964, being cut up at a local scrap yard very soon afterwards.

(*Les Hanson*)

137. Railway photographers, standing in the freezing cold hour after hour in pursuit of their hobby, pray for one, just one, unusual occurrence to make the sojourn worthwhile, and on 28 March 1963 Ken Fairey's prayers were answered when the most unlikely combination of an A4 Pacific and a coal train appeared in his viewfinder! Such workings did occasionally take place, usually after works visits or at times of locomotive failure, but they were nevertheless extremely rare and one could easily have stood alongside the East Coast Main Line once a week for 30 years and still not witnessed such a spectacle. The locomotive in question is No. 60008 "Dwight D. Eisenhower", and this up coal working was captured on film approaching Sandy. At the time most ECML expresses were in the hands of 'Deltic' and Brush Type 4 (later class 47) diesels, and although "Dwight D. Eisenhower" (formerly the celebrated "Golden Shuttle") was still officially a member of the King's Cross top-link, withdrawal was only four months away. It is possible, therefore, that 'Top Shed' had sadly already run out of passenger work for its once illustrious 'Streak'.   (*Ken Fairey*)

138. From the ridiculous to the sublime! If ever a class of locomotive was suited to a coal train, it was the remarkable 2-8-2 'Booster' engines of class P1. Designed by Gresley and built in 1925, these Mikados were intended to be the 'Pacifics of the goods train fleet'. Indeed, Gresley even fitted them with Pacific boilers virtually identical to those he was using on the A1s (later A3s). To make the locos even more powerful, he provided a steam-powered booster engine on the trailing axle, the pipe and exhaust of which can easily be made out under the cab. The idea was to haul gargantuan loads of coal from New England to Ferme Park without the need to double-head, but although the two engines built (Nos. 2393 and 2394) proved themselves superbly capable, they also proved that Gresley's genius was sometimes *too* great, for the length of trains they were able to haul was too long to fit into many of the signalling blocks of the time! As a result, the P1s became under-utilised, the boosters were removed in 1937/38 and both locomotives were withdrawn in 1945, victims of their own success. No. 2393 is seen heading south at Sandy, running alongside the ex-LNWR line from Bletchley to Cambridge.   (*Soole Collection/National Railway Museum*)

139. LNER J3 class 0-6-0 No. 4100 plods its way in workmanlike fashion along the foot of the sandstone escarpment at Sandy on Saturday 1 May 1937. The J3s are somewhat notable in that the class was turned out by no fewer than four different manufacturers: Doncaster, Vulcan Foundry, Kitson & Co. and Dübs & Co., No. 4100 being by Dübs, leaving that company's Glasgow plant in March 1898 as a class J4. It was rebuilt as a J3 by the GNR in November 1918 and survived until June 1952, although it never actually carried its allotted BR number: 64117. The first wagon in the train of private-owner coal and anthracite wagons announces that its Swansea-based owner purveys the 'best anthracite, steam and house coals'. Now, South Wales – once synonymous with coal – possesses not a single British Coal deep mine, while private-owner wagons, after a long nationalised interregnum, are once again the norm. It's a strange old world.   (Les Hanson)

140. Nothing was more calculated to get the adrenalin flowing than the sight of a silver 'Streak' in full cry, as in the eyes of all but the most ardent Crewe or Swindon fan, these magnificent locomotives represented the pinnacle of British express passenger steam locomotive development. Although the A4 class numbered 35 examples at its peak (one was destroyed in a wartime air raid on York shed), only the first four boasted silver-grey livery – Nos. 2509 "Silver Link", 2510 "Quicksilver", 2511 "Silver King" and 2512 "Silver Fox" – and "Quicksilver" was less than two years old when this striking photograph was taken of an up express at Sandy on the same day as the picture opposite. Whether the children of today will grow up to regard HSTs and 91s with similar affection is open to debate. *(Les Hanson)*

141. "Flying Scotsman" on the 'Flying Scotsman'. It wasn't all that often that No. 4472 was rostered to work the train of the same name, but an early instance was recorded here at Sandy round about 1933 by that doyen of pre-war action photographers G.H. Soole. He is standing under the LNWR flyover at Girtford, looking back towards Sandy Station, and just showing under the road bridge are the buffer-stops of the GN siding which never saw much use, and which was to be removed before the end of WWII. The somersault signal did not outlast the war either, and it is to be wondered how long the gentleman on the left was allowed to stand in this position reading his newspaper! Since he's showing no interest in what's going on behind him, perhaps we can assume that maybe he's just picked the winner in the 2.30.

(*G.H. Soole/Geoff Goslin collection*)

142. In exactly the same position as the picture opposite, B1 4-6-0 No. 61279 hurries through Sandy with a down Cleethorpes express in August, 1962. To the left are the sand-hills, so popular with train-spotters, giving as they did at the time a completely unrestricted view of the line from the Girtford flyover (north) right round to Sandy Station (south). After mid-morning, the sun gets quite wrong for effective photography, and today one can hardly see the line at all from the top because of the unhindered growth of a multitude of trees, shrubs and bushes. But right up to the end of steam, there was hardly a spotter from anywhere in this part of England who didn't make a regular pilgrimage up the sand-hills for a frequent 'fix' of passing V2s, A3s and A4s. *(Geoff Goslin)*

143. The streamlined A4 Pacifics reigned supreme on the East Coast Main Line prestige services from the mid-1930s to the early 1960s; Gresley's masterpieces *indeed*. Approaching Tempsford Station during the summer of 1953, A4 4-6-2 No. 60028 "Walter K. Wigham" (formerly "Sea Eagle") is well into its stride as it speeds 'The Elizabethan' express non-stop over the 392^3/$_4$ miles between King's Cross and Edinburgh Waverley. The King's Cross men are in charge here, and the Haymarket crew, now sitting comfortably in the first compartment of the second coach, will walk through the corridor tender (see picture 146) just north of York and relieve the King's Cross crew for the remainder of the journey to the Scottish capital. Two miles north of Tempsford Station this named train will cross over the border from Bedfordshire to Huntingdonshire, then onward to Peterborough where its 95 mph running will be brought down to 25 mph as it crawls through the severe curves of that station. Today's trains suffer no such restriction following much track realignment in the early 1970s.

(Geoff Goslin)

144. Everton is best known throughout the land as one of the nation's top football teams having, at the time of writing, just won the 1995 FA Cup, but to the inhabitants of east Bedfordshire, Everton is a hamlet to the south-east of Tempsford, boasting a level crossing and fine girder footbridge over the four-track East Coast Main Line. In sleeveless sweaters on an August day in 1951, three young enthusiasts admire the passage of filthy WD 2-8-0 No. 90239 as it plods by with a long train of wooden-bodied coal wagons. This particular 'Austerity' spent its entire BR life operating out of New England shed in Peterborough, doubtless on trains just such as this. How many Bedfordshire spotters who yelled 'Scrap it!' after seeing it for the umpteenth time in those far-off days now bitterly regret their suggestion? *(Geoff Goslin)*

145. The project to construct an all-new Peppercorn A1 Pacific at Darlington in the 1990s certainly caught the imagination, and the thought of one of these majestic machines in action again persuaded donors from all over the country to contribute to the scheme. Captured entering St Neots Station on an up express on Monday 23 April 1962 is York shed's A1 No. 60154 "Bon Accord", one of the original members of this fine class, all scandalously scrapped in the '60s despite being less than 20 years old at the time. St Neots, although not quite in Bedfordshire, lies roughly midway between Sandy and Huntingdon, and despite being a sizeable market town, never possessed a railway junction with neighbouring communities. In this glimpse of the past, note the swan-neck gas lamps, tall home signals and somewhat unusual 'off-centre' positioning of the loco's shedplate. Although a footstep at the bottom of the smokebox door was a feature of the A1s, the usual position of the shedplate was in the centre, beneath the lower doorstrap. *(Ken Fairey)*

146. Heading south towards the Bedfordshire border, A4 4-6-2 No. 60017 "Silver Fox" clearly displays the cast fox on the side of the boiler cladding as 'The Northumbrian' climbs the last few yards of 1 in 200 towards St Neots Station on Thursday 19 July 1962, and from this angle the round window at the end of the corridor down the side of the tender can clearly be seen. This facility for changing crews on the move was solely devoted to 'The Elizabethan' at this time, so the Top Shed crew in charge of "Silver Fox" would have worked north to Newcastle the day before, lodged overnight, and then brought their A4 the 268 miles back from Newcastle to London on this train. The engine has a fine head of steam, the fireman is taking it easy in his cab seat watching the track ahead and, with just 52 miles to go, the train should be in King's Cross within the hour.

(*Ken Fairey*)

147. For the first 127 years of its existence the WCML did not encroach at all upon the county of Bedfordshire. Oh, yes, there had long been a station called 'Leighton Buzzard', but Leighton Buzzard Station had always been in Linslade, and until the alteration of the county boundary here in 1965, Linslade was in Buckinghamshire, as was the railway. Even today the WCML struggles to stay within the confines of the county for more than about three miles, but into Bedfordshire it assuredly now comes, and therefore provides us with an excuse to include the stretch of line from near Cheddington (Great Train Robbery country) through Bletchley and on to Wolverton. Opened as the London & Birmingham Railway in 1838, it became the LNWR in 1846, and the LMS at the grouping in 1923. Running through very level countryside, the only major constructions are the short parallel tunnels at Linslade. It was on this line that Stanier's masterpieces, the streamlined Princess Coronation class Pacifics of 1937 were put through their record-breaking paces. Much later, in the 1950s, the BR Standard classes appeared, displacing most of the earlier more interesting locomotives. Working hard on the up slow line, class G2a 7F No. 49078 moves a long Bletchley Yard to Leighton Buzzard local goods train south near Old Linslade on Saturday 14 April 1962. (*S. Summerson*)

148. The largest BR Standard class (251 locomotives), designed by Riddles, first appeared in 1954 for heavy goods duties, and was the hugely successful 9F class of 2-10-0s. Consequently they were something of a novelty on passenger workings, and could generally be guaranteed railway press coverage when such events were recorded. The author was fortunate to be on hand here with his camera to capture No. 92114 heading north on the main line near Leighton Buzzard with a troop-train composed largely of ex-Southern Railway stock one day during the summer of 1959. The driver is watching the road ahead intently and, given the main line situation and the obvious speed of the train, one of his concerns must be the frequency at which those little 5 ft. diameter driving-wheels are whirling round. (*David Eatwell*)

149. Spectacularly negotiating the reverse curves away from Linslade Tunnel, WD class 2-8-0 No. 90437 is romping into Leighton Buzzard Station on Saturday afternoon 3 November 1951. A puff of chalk-dust hits the six-foot way as the sheeted-over wagons' cargo finds cracks in the timbers, and with both the home and distant signals above the first wagons 'off', this ex-War Department loco, purchased by British Railways in 1948, is well on course for Cheddington and Tring Stations next. (*Harold Clements*)

150. A timeless study taken from the footbridge spanning all the tracks just south of Leighton Buzzard Station. The date is mid-June 1949 and the locomotive is ex-LNWR 0-8-0 Super D No. 9427. There were 502 in the class, and a few were kept at Leighton Buzzard to work the heavy sand and lime trains from the Totternhoe Lime Company's sidings off the Dunstable branch beyond Stanbridgeford. The scene is now an elongated commuter-car-park.

(Harold Clements)

151. (above) and 152. (opposite) The engine shed at Leighton Buzzard provided motive power not only for local goods workings up and down the West Coast Main Line, but also for services along the LNWR branch to Dunstable. A modest two-road brick-built affair with arched entrances in pre-Grouping and LMS days (above), by the time the picture opposite was taken it had been shortened (losing the arches in the process) and re-roofed in corrugated cladding. Local quarries producing chalk and sand kept the depot busy for many years, and by the mid-1950s more than half a dozen locomotives were sub-shedded here from the parent depot at Bletchley, one being a six-coupled tank loco for passenger work and the rest ex-LNWR 0-8-0 heavy goods engines, such as class G2 Nos. 49005, 49122 and 49139, seen on August Bank Holiday Monday 1955. By the time the shed rebuilding work had been carried out in 1957, Stanier 8F 2-8-0s had begun to supplement the venerable G2s, but a fine old loco in the shape of No. 49093 (opposite) was still to be found in steam here on Saturday 15 July 1961. In the end, the demise of the old 'Super Ds' effectively spelt the end for the depot, and it closed in November 1962.

(above S. Summerson, opposite R.J. White)

153. Super D class G2a 0-8-0 No. 48914 is positively storming through Leighton Buzzard at 14.35 on the up slow line with a southbound goods train bound for London on Monday 23 April 1951. The BR number on the cab-side is done in block-style numerals, and the locomotive hails from 4B, Northampton. To the right, the LMS style 'Leighton Buzzard' station sign proclaims 'Change for Dunstable and Luton Branch', and do note the two sand containers on the platform awaiting use by staff. A nice touch.   (*Harold Clements*)

154. At first glance, Princess Royal 4-6-2 No. 46207 "Princess Arthur of Connaught" is speeding southbound through Leighton Buzzard on the up main with an express, but a more detailed look reveals class C headlamps over the buffer beam and the train consisting of a real mix of coaches and parcels vans. The date is Saturday 15 July 1961, and No. 46207, displaced from named-train duties by new diesels, is seeing out its last days in revenue earning service on more mundane tasks on the up slow line! To the right, beyond the gentleman in the white shirt, is the line to Dunstable, the locomotive there being made ready to head back along the branch later in the day.　　　　(R.J. White)

155. With a flurry of steam and noise, Princess Coronation class 4-6-2 No. 46240 "City of Coventry" speeds northwards past Leighton No. 1 signal box and through the station, en route, perhaps, to Crewe, with an un-named express train on Saturday 28 April 1962. A labour-intensive permanent way gang is busily occupied on the up slow line crossing, and in the sidings in the background can be seen many wagons filled with chalk from the Totternhoe Lime Company's quarry workings off the Dunstable branch, which curves away to the east on a slightly lower level. About 10 weeks after the date of this photograph, on 2 July 1962 the branch line to Dunstable was closed completely and the chalk traffic lost to the railway forever when a pipeline to carry the slurried chalk from Dunstable to Southam was put into use by the Rugby Portland Cement Co. It is still doing the same job today.

(*S. Summerson*)

156. Passing the same spot as sister loco "City of Coventry" opposite, No. 46253 "City of St Albans" hurries through Leighton Buzzard Station with the northbound 'Shamrock' express from Euston to Liverpool Lime Street on Saturday 14 April 1962. On the left is the loco depot which has lost part of its roof (see picture 151), and above the Pacific sits another line of wagons full of chalk, recently arrived from Totternhoe. On weekdays 'The Shamrock' departed Euston at 16.55 and ran non-stop to Liverpool, arriving in Lime Street at 20.35. Here passengers could embark on the Belfast Steamship Co. vessel to Belfast, or the British & Irish Steam Packet Co. boat to Dublin. Whereas the weekday northbound service ran non-stop, the Saturday service stopped at Rugby and Crewe, and every day of the week the southbound 'Shamrock' stopped at Runcorn, Crewe and Bletchley!   (S. Summerson)

157. A fine panorama of Bedfordshire and Buckinghamshire scenery can be seen from above the northern portals of Linslade Tunnels, as rebuilt Patriot 4-6-0 No. 45534 "E. Tootal Broadhurst" rushes a long express towards the up main bore and the sharp curves through Leighton Buzzard Station on Saturday afternoon, 4 August 1962. The forerunners of the railways in Great Britain were the waterways, and above the third coach and this bridge can be seen the Grand Union Canal, lazily meandering its way northwards between the main line and, just across the field, the River Ouzel. The road bridge carries the Leighton Buzzard to Bletchley road across the railway, and two miles further north, close to Milepost 43, it does the same thing again.

(S. Summerson)

158. With a tender well-filled with coal, Jubilee class 4-6-0 No. 45740 "Munster" gallops out of the north end of Linslade Tunnel on the down slow line with a fully-fitted fast goods train on the same day as the facing photograph. It is a very hot sunny day, causing no exhaust to be visible from No. 45740 which, with silver painted smokebox door hinges and in pleasantly clean condition, looks to have been on a special working recently. Linslade Tunnels boast an awkward combination of small and large bores, and the engineers involved in the planning of the forthcoming 25kv railway were, at this time, even contemplating the elimination of the tunnels and making a deep cutting. This option was not implemented, and instead the tracks through the single line tunnels were lowered to take the overhead catenary. This fine castellated portico marks the entrance to the cavernous depths that 'Ossie' Nock so graphically refers to in his foreword.   (S. Summerson)

159. Just over a mile south of Bletchley, Princess Royal class 4-6-2 No. 46207 "Princess Arthur of Connaught" speeds towards Euston with the up 'Ulster Express', whilst behind it, on the slow line, an 8F 2-8-0 heads south on a long goods train, and will be within perfect camera range in another minute or two. The tracks to the left of the picture were known as Lamb's Sidings, and after access through the gate, struck away for about half a mile in a north-westerly direction to brickworks, now long demolished. (See picture161) *(David Eatwell)*

160. Sheer LMS elegance manifests itself as unrebuilt and un-named Patriot class 4-6-0 No. 45547 heads north on a fully fitted class C goods train during a summer's afternoon in 1959. The Patriot has a fine head of steam in hand as it approaches Bletchley, and the bars on that lovely old tender are certainly needed to keep the huge load of coal provided by Willesden Loco Depot safe and intact. Based on an original 1930 Fowler design, this locomotive was built in 1933 as a new unit, whereas some of the earlier numbered Patriots were in fact rebuilds of original LNWR Claughton class locomotives.

(*David Eatwell*)

161. Two birds (of the feathered variety) wing their way diagonally across the West Coast Main Line north of Bletchley as pilot locomotive Black Five 4-6-0 No. 45418 and train locomotive rebuilt Patriot 4-6-0 No. 45521 "Rhyl" scurry southwards with a huge 15-coach express from the North Wales holiday resorts bound for Euston. Lamb's Sidings signalman has pulled off his down main home signals, heralding movement on the adjacent track, but Bletchley South still has to accept the train, thus the distant signals are still firmly 'On'. Beyond our airborne friends, on the southern outskirts of Bletchley are the huge chimneys pinpointing the London Brick Company's site, now the beautifully landscaped Blue Lagoon and Country Park. Above the train the whole area has been unrecognisably transformed by the building of a large modern housing estate.

(*David Eatwell*)

162.When the author climbed up the embankment from the road below one day in the summer of 1959 (armed with his trusty Retina IIIc loaded with HP3 film and with his lineside photographic permit easily accessible in his pocket), little did he expect to find the spot he had selected to spend his lunch-hour occupied by these two young trespassers on the grass verge! (Will they recognise themselves today, more than 35 years later, one wonders?) Beyond the train is the Bletchley flyover (locally known as the 'White Elephant'), with the south signals showing prominently above it, and in front of the train, loaded wagons wait in the coal yard. Of the train itself, one can but surmise the reason for Rugby's un-rebuilt Patriot No. 45533 "Lord Rathmore" piloting the Edge Hill Jubilee No. 45704 "Leviathan" on just a 12-coach train to Euston; not that the Patriot, its injector obviously in use, seems to be giving a great deal of assistance to the much harder working Jubilee!

(David Eatwell)

163. Bletchley Station, well established in Buckinghamshire yet only just beyond the Bedfordshire border, lies 46 miles from Euston, and is the junction for the Oxford and Bedford (and Cambridge) lines. Here, on Saturday 3 May 1958, LMS class 5 4-6-0 No. 45195 is about to depart with a short train to Bicester and Oxford. How nice it is to see a genuine old LNWR signal still extant in 1958, and it is noted that the Black Five's tender still carries the early 1950s 'Ferret and Dartboard' BR totem.

(*S. Summerson*)

164. Stopped in the up main platform at Bletchley Station on Saturday 9 April 1955, Princess Coronation class 4-6-2 No. 46251 "City of Nottingham" is at the head of the massively long 'Shamrock' express from Liverpool, impatiently awaiting the 'off' for Euston. Stops at Bletchley in this era were frequently somewhat prolonged affairs, caused as often as not by the fact that trains such as this could overlap the platforms by as many as six or eight coaches, and the antics of station staff frantically waving to the footplate during the drawing-up manoeuvres, caused much mirth amongst the usual merry band of bystanders. Ah! – memories, memories. (*S. Summerson*)

165. (left) A fascinating look at Bletchley Station buildings on the west side of the main lines in pre-1923 LNWR days. A row of locomotives can be seen beyond the station on the motive power depot, and the station gardens to the left were a regular feature in those long-ago days.
(*Bernard Matthews Collection*)

166. (below) Bletchley Station, viewed from the south, in 1908. The photographer is standing in the middle of the up main line, and on the same track a coach is at the far end of the platform. Milk churns and wicker baskets await a stopping train at the up slow platform, and here in these pre-Word War I years it can easily be appreciated what an important junction had been established at Bletchley.
(*Bernard Matthews Collection*)

167. (left) An exterior view of Bletchley Station in about 1900, at a time when Milton Keynes was just a very small village and the railway station was the focal point of most provincial towns. The building straight ahead was the Post Office, and behind the gentleman sitting upon his horse-and-trap combination is the refreshment room, no doubt accessible from both the station platform and the courtyard. Excursions and bargain fares were as much a feature of Victorian life as they are today, and the posters within the main station entrance were intended to catch the eye of passengers at the turn of the century.

(*Bernard Matthews Collection*)

168. (right) Positive LNWR hardware at Bletchley loco depot on Wednesday 15 June 1938. No. 25797 was a member of the Prince of Wales 4P class of 4-6-0s designed by B. Cooke in 1911, and although this particular locomotive was scrapped soon after World War II, there were 22 of them still left on the LMS in 1943. When all the railways merged on 1 January 1948, six of the class actually made it to the state system and four of them were allocated the numbers 58000-58003, but in the event, did not carry them. They were No. 25648 "Queen of the Belgians", No. 25673 "Lusitania", No. 25752 and No. 25787. The other two, Nos. 25722 and 25827 were never allocated BR numbers, but "Lusitania" became a much loved (and eventually much missed) performer on the Oxford-Cambridge line through Bedford, as did the outside valve-geared No. 25845 which lasted until 1947, and was known affectionately to local footplatemen as 'Tishy'. (*J.M. Jarvis*)

169. A classic LNWR locomotive pose at Bletchley Station showing Teutonic class 3-cylinder compound 2-4-0 No. 1353 "City of Edinburgh" pausing with an express on the up main in the early 1900s. During the famous 'Races to the North' in 1895, it was this class of locomotive which was used on the Euston to Crewe section of the high-speed journey to Aberdeen, acquitting itself with great credit and winning many plaudits for its performance along the way.

(*Tripp Collection/National Railway Museum*)

170. Interesting detail is shown of un-rebuilt Patriot class 4-6-0 No. 45533 "Lord Rathmore" whilst it pauses in the down slow platform at Bletchley Station during the summer of 1959. It is at the head of a stopping train from Euston to Northampton and, if nothing else, it could certainly do with a good clean and some spit and polish! The shed plate tells us that "Lord Rathmore" was allocated to 2A Rugby MPD at this time, yet three years later, in September 1962, it was withdrawn for scrap from Edge Hill MPD, Liverpool. Perhaps a good clean might have saved it to become the only one of its class to be preserved; the lack of an un-rebuilt Patriot being often remarked upon as a serious gap in today's preservation movement.

(David Eatwell)

171. Just pulling away from Bletchley and heading north is rebuilt Jubilee class 4-6-0 No. 45735 "Comet" in the summer of 1960. One of only two Jubilee locomotives to carry a higher traffic rating, "Comet" was rebuilt in 1942 with a larger boiler and a double chimney, then having more the appearance of a rebuilt Patriot than a Jubilee. Beyond the locomotive we can see part of Bletchley Loco Depot as it was when it carried the code 1E; solid and permanent looking, yet destined to close only five years later, during 1965. *(David Eatwell)*

172. The home and distant signals are well and truly 'off' for Royal Scot class 4-6-0 No. 46154 "The Hussar" as it awaits the right away signal from the guard at Bletchley Station, about the same date as the previous picture. "The Hussar's" fireman nonchalantly studies the scenery to the east of Bletchley Station, blissfully unaware that the cap atop his tender's water filler hole is in its raised position, so that when he lowers the water scoop over Castlethorpe Troughs some eight miles down the line, the water being picked up will shoot spectacularly sky-high and be blown back over the carriages to the consternation of all within! Note, too, the point rodding between the tracks, guided along the sides of redundant lengths of rail. No doubt it is a long pull from the signal box, and the 'guides' will help to maintain the rigidity of the rodding over the elongated distance. Compare the locos on these two pages; they are in the same spot and look the same (well, almost) but are of completely different classes.

(*David Eatwell*)

173. Designed by F.W. Webb for the LNWR in 1898, class 2P 0-6-2T No. 6900 looks in immaculate condition shunting at Bletchley Loco Depot on Saturday 29 May 1937. There were 80 members of this class originally constructed, yet by 1943 only 30 remained, and by 1948 they had been whittled down to just 15 under the British Railways banner. This particular example, with the number 46900 was the very last member of the class to be scrapped in 1953.

(*J.M. Jarvis*)

174. A splendid study of an elegant locomotive. Nicely cleaned and looking impeccably smart, un-named Patriot class 4-6-0 No. 5545, not yet four years old, rests outside Bletchley shed on Saturday 29 May 1937. The 9A shed plate announces that it is a Longsight loco from Manchester, and above it, W912 tells us that No. 5545 has worked into Bletchley on a special excursion; it having been turned and coaled now, ready for the return journey to the north later in the day. In Bedfordshire, the word 'Patriot' was always pronounced with the first syllable rhyming with 'hat' and not, as the Americans do, rhyming it with 'hate'. Hence the local nickname for the class – 'Pats'. Although there were 52 locos in the class and the highest number was 5551, No. 5545 was actually the last one to be delivered. Perhaps somebody at the LMS just wasn't very good at counting in 1934!

(J.M. Jarvis)

175. Sporting a 24E (Blackpool) shedplate, Jubilee class 4-6-0 No. 45653 "Barham" pulls away from Bletchley Station on a northbound, Saturdays Only train, in September 1959. With Gresley teak-bodied-and-beaded coaches as the first and third vehicles of the train, and the remainder being largely BR Mark I stock, the train has all the trappings of a once-a-week set. The locomotive had worked up to London from Blackpool earlier, and is now taking the same set back on this rather grey and overcast Saturday afternoon. *(David Eatwell)*

176. A magnificent period cameo depicting the scene at Bletchley engine shed on Tuesday 4 September 1917, the substantial six-road depot having been built in 1873 to replace a flimsy wooden structure which a gale had blown down the year before. At the time of this photograph, Bletchley was home to 60 locos (46 working from base with 14 at sub-sheds) and provided traction not only for goods trains, but also for the Oxford, Cambridge and London locals. Among the handsome LNWR engines visible are Precedent 2-4-0 No. 506 "Sir William Cockburn" and George V 4-4-0 No. 1799 "Woodcock". Bletchley shed was closed on 5 July 1965 and was soon demolished, although the town – now part of the sprawling Milton Keynes City complex – still possesses some sort of shed in the form of Bletchley Traction Maintenance Depot. The stone wall on the right, here supporting ash-disposal wheelbarrows, consists of rows of early sleeper blocks and is retained to this day beside the car park, although it is doubtful if many commuters realise the historical significance of what they are bumping their cars into!

(*National Railway Museum*)

177. (above) and 178. (below) At Wolverton was the LNWR carriage works. Chosen because of its location half way between London and Birmingham, at first it was also that company's main engine-repair depot, but by 1845 it was turning out its first locomotives: a pair of Bury 2-2-0s. Carriage-building continued alongside engines for more than 30 years, and in fact the first locomotive in Australia was a product of Wolverton. It still exists, and is a 0-4-2; the only McConnell loco to be preserved anywhere in the world. By 1877 Crewe had become fully established as the LNWR locomotive building depot, and Wolverton's dual role changed to concentrate solely on carriage construction, eventually becoming one of the leaders in this field worldwide. Our own royal train came from here, and an example of Wolverton's early construction prowess is Queen Adelaide's saloon carriage of 1842, now on display at the NRM in York. As the works expanded, so it became necessary for Wolverton to employ its own shunting engines, and the first of these arrived in 1877, to be followed at intervals by two similar small tank engines, and then, in 1895, by a pair of Crewe-built 0-4-2 crane tanks. But it was the collection of four Ramsbottom 0-6-0 saddle tanks which made a visit to Wolverton so important for so many enthusiasts. The first of these memorable machines arrived in June 1896, and they were here until 1959, although CD1 was taken out of service in 1937 to be replaced by the only one to carry a name: CD8 "Earlestown". The picture below shows CD3 of 1880 during a works visit on Saturday 19 April 1958, just 16 months before withdrawal, and the picture above is of one of the replacement locos used until diesels took over at the end of 1960. Bletchley shed provided Wolverton's last steam locos, and No. 27496, a 0-6-0 special tank (rebuilt from a tender engine) was one of them, seen outside the works with Wolverton No. 1 signal box behind it.

(Above *R.G. Jarvis*, below *H.C. Casserley*)

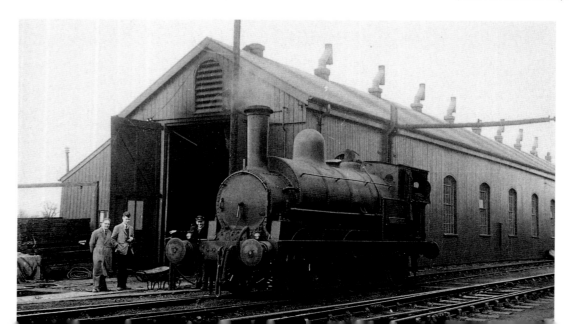

179. Only two street tramway systems have ever been installed in this area; one was at Luton (see picture 64) and the other ran between Wolverton, Stony Stratford and (for a while) Deanshanger. The gauge was 3 ft. 6 in., and the 'main' line was a little over 2½ miles long, the short-lived Deanshanger extension of 1899 adding a further two miles to the route distance. Founded in 1885, the Stony Stratford & District Light Railway Company opened for business the following year, connecting Wolverton Station with the Barley Mow in Stony Stratford, although for many years the two termini were the cattle sidings and 'The Cock Inn' respectively. Motive power was mostly in the hands of 'conventional' steam tram locomotives; two manufacturers being employed by the company. They were the German makers Krauss and Britain's Thomas Green, but for the last five years of its existence, the line also saw a 1921-built 0-4-0ST by Bagnall supplementing the original stud. Derailments were frequent. Half a dozen passenger cars were utilised, ranging in size from a 120-seater to a 20-seater, and three or four goods wagons, but by 1926 traffic had dwindled to such an extent that non-profitability forced closure, and today not a single sign remains to remind passers by of the Wolverton Steam Tram, shown here awaiting custom on the bridge outside Wolverton's wooden station building.

(Tripp/National Railway Museum)

THE NORTHAMPTON BRANCH
OLNEY TO BEDFORD

180. Fowler-designed LMS 4F 0-6-0 No. 44317 of Bedford, adorns the turntable at Olney on Thursday 27 June 1957. The former Stratford-upon-Avon & Midland Junction line through Fenny Compton and Towcester joined the Bedford to Northampton line at Ravenstone Wood Junction via a south-east facing connection mid-way between Olney and Piddington, and in the early 1890s the MR provided loco servicing facilities at Olney in the shape of a small locomotive shed (used by the S&MJR), a water tower and a turntable, all visible in this view. Passenger traffic over the eastern section of the S&MJR had ceased in April 1893, but the line saw heavy use during World War II and was useful for some cross-country goods movements, including the shipment of bananas from Avonmouth Docks to London until the outbreak of war in 1939, although the loco servicing facilities at Olney were still in use, despite having been officially 'closed' since 1928! The final passenger train ran on Saturday 3 March 1962.

(*Ken Fairey*)

181. The handsome exterior facade of Olney Station in Buckinghamshire in the earliest years of the twentieth century. Built for the line's opening on 10 June 1872, it had an imposing local stone cottage-style shape with delightful gabled windows, solid chimneys and a tiled porch. Unlike all the other stations along this 20-mile-long branch line, Olney's was very conveniently placed near the town centre and boasted quite a healthy amount of commuter traffic into both Bedford and Northampton, although off-peak hours were very quiet indeed. All traces of the building have now disappeared under new developments within Olney town, but it was, in fact, virtually identical to the station at Turvey (see picture 185) which happily still exists.   (*Derek Cockings Collection*)

182. Johnson Midland Railway Victorian-built 3F 0-6-0 No. 43665, as rebuilt in 1924, trundles a short goods train along the Northampton to Bedford branch on Saturday 25 July 1959. Milepost 57 was situated close to the village of Newton Blossomville, about a mile to the west of Turvey Station, and this vintage 1885 locomotive presents an idyllic scene in the shallow tree-lined cutting, totally unaware of the decimation that our beloved railway system would witness in the 'swinging sixties'! Already bereft of its shed plate when caught on camera here, No. 43665 had been withdrawn by the end of the year, a veteran of nearly 75 summers.

(*Tom Rounthwaite/J. Parker Collection*)

183. (right) and 184. (below) There is a plateau of high ground, about 350 ft. above sea level, between Bedford and Northampton known as Yardley Chase and, whilst the resulting inclines on the branch line gave little trouble to the passenger services, goods trains often struggled and the local enginemen spoke of 'going over the Alps' between the two county towns. On 31 July 1960, the driver of Stanier 8F 2-8-0 No. 48616 misunderstood instructions given him by the signalman, and ran into a line of stored coaches. The accident happened near Turvey Station, and the 8F came to grief in spectacular fashion at the bottom of an embankment, its load of 60 ft. lengths of track spilling all over the site as the flat bogie wagons piled up behind the wrecked locomotive. Recovery of the Cricklewood-allocated 8F was a major task involving two huge rail-mounted cranes, and No. 48616 was officially withdrawn on 22 October 1960, being deemed too badly damaged to warrant repair.

(*Both pictures: Ken Fairey*)

185. Ivatt LMS taper boiler class 2 2-6-2T No. 41224 pauses at Turvey Station en route from Northampton to Bedford with one of the last trains to run before the final withdrawal of passenger services. The actual closure date was Saturday 3 March 1962, a grey overcast day befitting the sad occasion, which saw all the trains well filled with passengers, and the last one crammed full of folk wishing to pay their last respects. The locomotive, No. 41225, was adorned with the usual wreath, and exploding detonators heralded the departure from each station. Opportunist printed notices stuck on the carriage windows proclaimed: 'Bedford-Northampton. Killed by the internal combustion engine. Farewell. RIP', and indeed this was the end of 90 years of faithful service to the local communities. The Ivatt 2-6-2Ts used on the line were all based at Bedford MPD, and normally operated at that end of their trains to facilitate servicing. Thus, facing Bedford, they pushed to Northampton and pulled on the way back. Ideally suited for branch line work, these useful little locomotives were introduced by the LMS in 1946 and were the standard motive power on the branch, their 5 ft. driving wheels proving ideal for frequent stopping and starting, and spirited running between stations. In the last years up to 1962, some of the new Standard class 2s in the 84000 series, fitted with push-pull equipment, were used, Nos. 84005/29 being shedded at Bedford. The former was one of the most commonly seen locos on both the Northampton and the Hitchin branches at the time, and the latter came from the Southern Region in 1961, having been displaced by the Kent electrification when only four years old.

(L. King)

186. A peaceful picture at Bedford as the driver of the Rail Motor, Stan Crawley, with the door of his cab slightly open, checks last minute details with the guard, Albert Smith, on Saturday 2 August 1958. LMS Ivatt designed 2-6-2T No. 41272, with a full head of steam, is shortly to leave for Northampton, and is at the business end of this locomotive-and-two-coaches set in 'The Dock' at the north end of Midland Road Station. This locomotive was the 5,000th built at Crewe works and was fitted with commemorative plaques on its side tanks. It came new to Bedford and later transferred to N. Devon. The mailbags on the platform trolley (right) have very likely come from the branch, and will soon be loaded aboard the next London-bound train at the adjacent platform.   (S. Summerson)

The 'Oxbridge' Line
Bletchley to Potton

187. Bedford's first railway. Not only the first in town, the Bedford-Bletchley branch was also the first railway in the whole county, and it was another two years before the next one arrived; also a branch off the LNW (the ex-London & Birmingham Railway) main line; this one to Dunstable. It was 17 November 1846 when the inaugural train ran on what was initially the Bedford Railway, but which had also become the LNWR by opening day, and the new station, later to be called St John's, was built in the part of the town then known as St Leonard's. The 'Railway Mania' was now getting under way with ambitious schemes being proposed almost daily, but few reached fruition; the next ones that came to the county being the Great Northern Railway (through Sandy) in 1850, the privately-owned Sandy & Potton Railway in 1857, and the Midland, running diagonally across Bedfordshire from just south of Wellingborough to just north of Hitchin. In 1862 the Bletchley-Bedford line was extended to Cambridge, and as Bletchley had been rail-connected with Oxford since 1851, the 'Oxbridge' line was now complete, and, with all their attractions, it is no small wonder that so much has been published about these 77 miles of cross-country railway in recent years. Not least has been the huge variety of steam locomotives which could be encountered; mainly Midland/LNWR/LMS classes, but GE/LNER types too, and, towards the end of steam on the branch, Standard classes up to 9Fs and Britannias in size. At the other end of the scale, often seen on charming little push-pull trains were members of the Midland 1P 0-4-4T class, like No. 1260 (above), here pushing two swing-step LNWR coaches out of Bletchley towards Bedford a year or two before the outbreak of World War II. A Bedford engine since 1932, No. 1260 was due to be renumbered 58037 by BR, but was scrapped in 1948 before this could be implemented. Between the two shunting signals, to the right of the picture, is the ex-L&Y 0-6-0ST No. 11505 of 1877, itself to be withdrawn in 1938, soon after being photographed here. Bletchley Shed (2B) is to the left of the locomotive and has since become a car park. *(Harold Clements)*

188. Bow Brickhill Halt, Saturday 3 May 1958, showing Black Five 4-6-0 No. 45187 of Willesden depot on an afternoon train from Bedford to Bletchley. It was not until the introduction of diesel services on the branch in 1959 that halts like Bow Brickhill had their platforms raised to standard heights, and here passengers are having to use the steps provided in order not to come a dreadful cropper when getting into or out of a coach. The brick building to the right of the train is not the station but the crossing keeper's house, and at one time there were 15 manned level crossings between Bedford and Bletchley. At night, with no rail traffic pending, it was usual for the gates to be closed against the trains at most crossings, but some gates (on the more minor roads) were set against road traffic, and a sure way of incurring the wrath of the keeper was to arrive by car at one of the crossings at 2 a.m. or so and ring the bell! And if the bell wasn't working (as was sometimes the case), the instructions were to sound the car horn! In these circumstances the keeper was not always as polite and cheerful as his employers would expect – I have been told! I can't imagine why.

(S. Summerson)

189.(above) and 190. (opposite) About half a mile from Lidlington in the direction of Bedford is the Marston Road crossing, complete, of course, with the crossing keeper's lodge. On Sunday 2 July 1961, BR brought into use only their second ever automatic half-barrier crossing, causing some consternation amongst the locals, who thought that this new-fangled contraption could not possibly be safe! Yet they need not have worried, as BR were thoughtful enough to include bi-lingual warning signs for the benefit of both the native Lidlingtonians and the hundreds of immigrant Italians who had come over for employment in the Bedfordshire brickworks following World War II. At Lidlington (as at Ridgmont) there were the Marston Valley Brickworks, whose products were in direct competition with those from the nearby (Stewartby) London Brick Co. Much output from both firms was transported by rail, but gradually road transport took over, the Marston Valley Brick Co's lorries being a distinctive orange colour and the London Brick Co's bright red. Following the takeover of the former by the latter we still saw plenty of heavily laden AECs, Fodens and ERFs struggling up Brogborough and Ampthill hills, but with the merger all these lorries became red, and another local institution had gone forever. In the picture above, LMS 2-6-0 'Crab' No. 42870 is heading towards Bedford with a gratifyingly long goods train, and opposite, could that be the official photographer's smart Austin A35 gracing the scene? Both pictures date from very soon after the new barriers had been installed.

(Both pictures: Butler/Webb Collection)

191. With the tall LNWR telegraph pole (absolutely bristling with ceramic insulators) towering above, 2-6-2T No. 41329 (15D) brings the 18.13 train from Bedford St John's to Bletchley into Stewartby Halt on Thursday 28 July 1955 – actually five minutes late, but then some things never change! The photographer was making the best possible use of the 'Vauxhall Fortnight' that year by capturing such engaging moments as this during his two-week annual holiday. Originally called Wootton Pillinge, Stewartby Halt still exists, but not in this form, the low wooden platforms having been raised to 'standard' height four years after this picture was taken, removing the 'wayside halt' feeling from Stewartby and giving it a well-deserved sense of greater importance. Most of the brickworks' chimneys are just out of the picture to the left, but five are prominent here, reminding us that this was the heyday of the brickmaking industry when Stewartby boasted 31 chimneys, and proudly proclaimed that it was 'The Biggest Brickworks in the World'. Today just eight chimneys remain, but by tomorrow it may be seven, and the next day – who knows?

(Harold Clements)

192. (right) Making its last public appearance before withdrawal, the specially spruced-up Fowler 2P 4-4-0 No. 40646 passes Bedford St John's No. 1 signal box light-engine on Saturday 14 April 1962. Generally similar to other Midland/LMS 4-4-0s of classes 2P, 3P and 4P (even those with outside cylinders), No. 40646 came from a class of 136 locos with 6 ft. 9 in. driving wheels which was introduced in 1928, and on this occasion was travelling to Luton Bute St via Bletchley (and the Leighton Buzzard branch) to rejoin the rail-tour it had brought into Bedford double-headed with the 3P 2-6-2T No. 40026 from Northampton (see pictures 270-273). Like almost everything else in this scene, the signal box is but a memory, having been burned down in 1977, subsequently being rebuilt in singularly unattractive style. The tall spire of St Paul's Church, to the left of the locomotive, can no longer be seen from this spot, being now obscured by tower blocks.

(S. Summerson)

193. (left) 4-6-0 on a goods. Northampton's Black Five No. 45147 has just passed under Ampthill Road bridge, Bedford, and is about to take the western leg of the St John's triangle to head towards Bletchley on Thursday 28 March 1963, just three years before steam finally finished at St John's. No. 45147, once a Bletchley engine, was regularly seen on the branch, and here will have come from St John's goods yard with this train of mixed wagons. The signal just behind the locomotive was the last lower quadrant arm (by a long way) in the Bedford area. More prominent in this view, though, are the tall flour mill (Pilgrim Animal Feeds), and the shorter chimney in Astell's woodyard. Behind the mill is St John's Station, and the line through it to Bletchley runs across the picture ahead of the locomotive. This section of line now sees use by the passenger trains between Bedford and Bletchley, but like the allotments (bottom right-hand corner), the other lines have gone, as have both the mill and woodyard; starter homes now occupy much of the area.

(Ken Fairey)

194. Here is a customary occurrence at Bedford St John's, with the loco fresh off the triangle, fetching the stock out of the centre road, prior to setting back into the platform and heading off up the line on a scheduled train to Bletchley. On this day, Saturday 7 November 1953, the departure was to be at 16.20, and the loco is one of the Standard class 4 4-6-0s, No. 75038. Four or five of the 80 class 4 locos built have been preserved, and one of these (often seen working) is No. 75069, a double-chimney version, based on the Severn Valley Railway at Bridgnorth. But surely, the station is as much the star of this scene as the loco. On the left, the bike shed sees heavy occupation both inside and out, and a little further along the platform, three fire buckets hang dutifully on the wall, everyone hoping, no doubt, that they will never have to be used in anger. They never were. Under the canopy, a trolley-load awaits entrainment, and yet more bicycles prop up the wall near the waiting room entrance. The right-hand platform was the original 'London Platform', dating back to when the line opened in 1846, hence the 'train shed' appearance; a left-over from the time when this was a terminus station and the main buildings were on this side of the station. At the time that the Cambridge extension was opened in 1862, these south-side buildings made way for the more opulent accommodation shown still in use on the north side, but they were knocked down some 10 years before St John's was finally phased out in May 1984, when trains were diverted to Bedford Midland.

(*T.J. Edgington*)

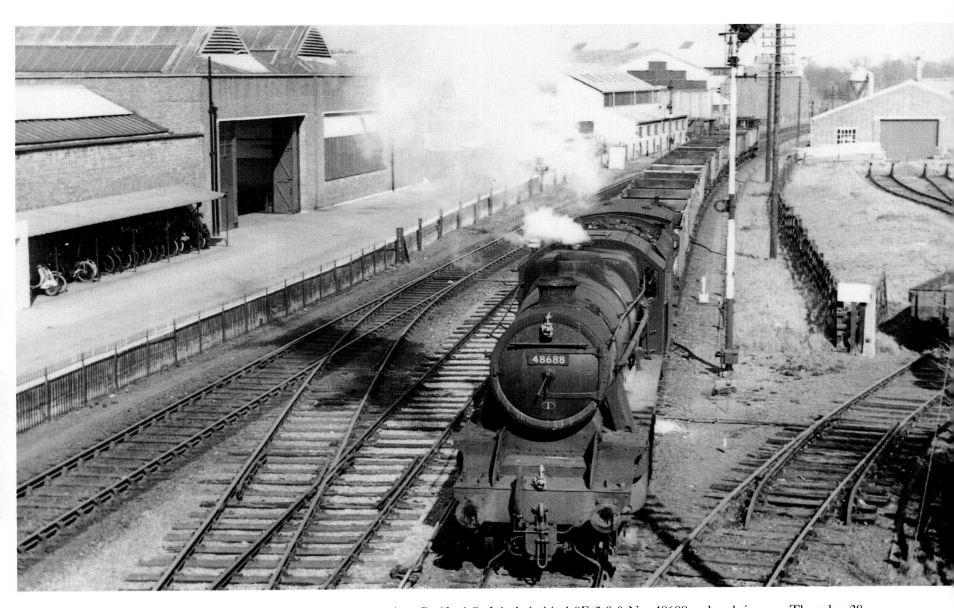

195. Goldington Power Station empty coal wagons ease into Bedford St John's behind 8F 2-8-0 No. 48688 at lunchtime on Thursday 28 March 1963. Steam was to continue on this duty for another three years, and even when the route to Sandy (and Cambridge) was closed in 1967, the service to the electricity generating station was maintained for another decade, albeit diesel hauled, of course. To view this scene, the photographer is standing on London Road bridge, looking at the United Counties bus garage (with obligatory bike shed) to the left, and just out of the picture on that side is the Railway Swan, the hostelry with the succession of interesting pub signs (see pictures 258 and 259). The sidings to the right served the Stirling Safway engineering works, now occupied by a DIY Superstore. *(Ken Fairey)*

196. The last station to open on the 'Oxbridge' line was Willington on 1 May 1903, although some halts (e.g. Girtford) did appear later. From the time the line was built, locals had strived to persuade the LNWR to give them their station (there had been a goods siding here for nine years) and eventually the company relented and the villagers got what they wanted – complete with the very latest type of signal box mounted on the down platform. Willington had an extra long passing loop, put in during World War I to accommodate the higher level of traffic using the line at that time, but today the route of a cycle-track passes through where the platforms were, and there is no hint that elegant structures such as this once graced the site with their stately presence.

(*Hugh Ramsey*)

197. (above) and 198. (below) Whereas Willington's station buildings always gave the impression of impermanence (the signal box excepted), at Blunham (above) it was just the opposite, and this is borne out by a visit here today, where the solid old LNWR building can be seen tastefully restored as a cosy modern residence. Everything else 'railway' has gone – rails, platforms, up-side shelter, signal box, goods shed, bridge, everything – and the fine old LNWR creation is somewhat incongruously enveloped in a modern housing estate. But the branch has been no stranger to modern developments. Amongst notable firsts was the St John's to Sandy single line section seeing the first ever use of an electric train-staff system (in 1888), and the whole 'Oxbridge' line hosting the first pneumatic-tyred vehicle ever to run on any of the country's railways (the Michelin rail-bus in 1932). Yet better known, perhaps, than either of these innovations was the beautiful red and cream Leyland diesel railcar set that was built by Sir William Stanier at Derby, and which went on trial on the branch in 1938. Seen at Blunham that summer (below), the three-car articulated train was quite luxurious, with both 1st and 3rd class accommodation, copious toilet facilities and seat backs which swivelled to allow passengers always to face the engine, like the street trams of the day. After leaving the branch, the combination went to the Midland Main Line from St Pancras, and was there at the outbreak of World War II, but experiments like this could not be continued in wartime, so the streamlined set was housed-up for a time in the old Midland shed at Bedford. Trials were never resumed, and parts of the set ended their days on electrification work for BR.   (Above *Bernard Matthews Collection*, Below *J.M. Jarvis*)

199. After crossing the East Coast Main Line at Girtford, the single line from Bedford fell at 1 in 125 for half a mile to reach Sandy, and on Thursday 28 March 1963 Black Five No. 45393 is rolling down the slope with a parcels train for Cambridge. The four tracks of the ECML are sweeping round on the left, but the line on the right is only a siding and not a through line, although it very rarely seemed to see much use.

(*Ken Fairey*)

200. The 4-4-0 wheel arrangement was as popular with British designers as it had been with those in America, and whichever region was preferred, observers would be almost certain to include a 4-4-0 in their list of favourite locos. With GWR fans, Dukes or Dukedogs might be the types; on the Southern it could be the Schools; LMS men would possibly point to the 2Ps, 3Ps and Compound 4Ps, but on the LNER they would be spoilt for choice. Alone among the Big Four, the LNER inherited more than a dozen different 4-4-0 classes at the grouping, and all of them great looking locos. There were Countys and Hunts, Scotts and Glens, Directors – and Claude Hamiltons. 4-4-0s somehow seemed to look just right, but inevitably some looked more 'right' than others, and the Claudes looked as right as rain! Introduced at the turn of the century, the D15 class (as it was then) was a Holden design for the Great Eastern, and eventually reached more than a hundred examples, including many rebuilds (which resulted in re-classification to D16). Details varied, but whether they had the large or small boiler (Belpaire or round-topped), slide valves or piston valves, short or extended smokeboxes, the Claude Hamilton 4-4-0s were as handsome a design as ever worked on Britain's railways, and viewers delighted in noting them regularly performing on the line from Cambridge. No. 62535, a D16/3 with piston valves and large round-topped boiler, was seen, shortly before withdrawal, leaving Sandy in August 1952 on a passenger working to Bedford, just about to cross over the ECML at Girtford. By 1960, sadly, the Claude Hamiltons had all gone.

(Geoff Goslin)

201. Stanier's development of a Fowler design, the 1935 4P 2-6-4T class eventually reached more than 200 machines, and so successful were they that they lasted virtually as long as steam itself on Britain's main railway lines. When BR needed tank engines of this size in the early '50s, what design did they choose? Why, this one of course; not exactly the same, but very similar, and it became the Standard class 4, preserved Nos. 80079 and 80080 of which have seen main line working in the 1990s. No. 2600, here leaving Sandy with an afternoon train from Cambridge to Bletchley on Saturday 1 May 1937, became No. 42600 in the BR renumbering scheme, but at this time still had the 1936-style numerals applied to both front and sides, and don't the oval buffers make a huge difference to the overall appearance?   (*Les Hanson*)

202. As fine a collection of private-owner wagons as you'll see in many a long day. The bottom train is on the East Coast Main Line, held at the 'peg' (signal), awaiting a path southwards through Sandy Station, and out of the picture to the left, more of the same; for some reason, on May Day 1937, nothing much moved on this track for some hours. On the LMS branch behind, the classic lines of the Prince of Wales 4-6-0 No. 25828 are well shown as it storms up the bank with a goods train for Bedford, very soon to cross the LNER line below, before completing the 10 miles into St John's, perhaps to take water in the station after regaining the double track, and then carrying on to Bletchley.

(Les Hanson)

203. At the same time as the mighty Midland Railway was cutting a swathe through central Bedfordshire with its initial drive towards London, a much less pretentious organisation was springing into life in the east of the county to connect the small market town of Potton with the Great Northern Main Line at the equally small market town of Sandy. Inevitably called the Sandy & Potton Railway, this privately built and owned four-mile line opened for passengers on 9 November 1857, initially possessing but a single locomotive – "Shannon" – bought new from George England of New Cross. This most attractive little 0-4-0WT worked throughout the five-year life of the line. Becoming part of the Bedford & Cambridge Railway in 1862, this new line was built using "Shannon" locally, which, when it was no longer needed here, was sold in 1878 and ended its working days on the Wantage Tramway (above), a short line not dissimilar to the Sandy & Potton Railway. It was the third son of Sir Robert Peel (of police fame) who had the Sandy & Potton Railway built while he was away on naval duty, but sadly Captain William Peel VC of the RSPB's Sandy Lodge (as it now is) never saw the results of his initiative, as he died in India from smallpox following the relief of Lucknow. In his honour, the little locomotive was named "Shannon" after the frigate he commanded. Today "Shannon" is based at Didcot, where it once worked, and as such is not only one of the most interesting locomotives preserved, it is also one of the oldest to have seen use in recent years. "Shannon's" shed, now a potato store on the outskirts of Potton, is the only building that remains to remind us of one of Bedfordshire's most imaginative schemes, the Sandy & Potton Railway. The photograph shows "Shannon" in wartime, crossing Grove Street, in Wantage.   (*National Railway Museum*)

LEIGHTON BUZZARD, DUNSTABLE AND LUTON (BUTE ST) TO LUTON HOO

204. Opened on 1 June 1848, the LNWR branch from Leighton Buzzard to Dunstable was never going to be one to make its owners rich, but it nevertheless carried satisfactory levels of goods and passenger traffic until the 1950s when increased road usage started to see off so many of the 'minor' railway lines. Its death knell finally sounded when the Totternhoe quarries decided to use alternative methods to transport their chalk and lime off site; the line finally closing to through goods trains on 1 January 1966. Historically, the line was a separate entity, and despite its end-on connection with the Great Northern from Hatfield, few through trains between Luton and Leighton Buzzard ran, even after nationalisation. Consequently, Dunstable (renamed Dunstable North from 1950) saw rolling-stock from the two large companies meeting here; e.g. N2s and, after 1923, N7s on the GN, and Duck 8s (Super Ds) on the LNWR. Level crossings proliferated, but there was no way round the Chilterns, so a gradient, as steep as 1 in 40, existed in the long cutting at Sewell, testing many an ageing locomotive to the limit. One such was No. 48953, shown here wheezing and clanking just over the summit with the regular 10 o'clock goods from Leighton Buzzard on Saturday 3 March 1961. A class with a very complicated history, these 0-8-0s date back to a Webb design of 1892, and members of the class have, over the years, had 2, 3 or 4 cylinders, and have been either simple or compound machines. Eventually totalling 502 locomotives, some even ran as 2-8-0s for up to 20 years, but were re-converted to 0-8-0s between 1917 and 1925. By the mid-'60s all had been withdrawn, with just one, No. 49395, preserved.
(Harold Clements)

205. Stanbridgeford Station, with its level crossing, first came into use, probably unofficially, in about 1849, but didn't appear in the Bradshaw timetable until November 1860 when the platforms were built, and right from the outset suffered the usual problems associated with so many stations at the time of being nowhere near the town (village/hamlet) it purported to serve! It *could* have been called Totternhoe, even, since it was equidistant from there and Stanbridge, but the name Stanbridgeford was probably thought to have a grander ring to it. A few commuters used the station, and occasionally there was a little military use, but any railway employee who fancied a quiet life would have been more than happy here. The 17.30 Saturday service from Leighton Buzzard, with its returning shoppers was a busier train than most, as evidenced here by the activity shown on the platform. The loco is 2P 2-6-2T No. 41289 and the date is 28 April 1962, just a couple of months prior to the withdrawal of passenger services on the branch, although quarry trains ran through until the middle of April, 1965.

(*S. Summerson*)

206. On Saturday 14 October 1961, 8F 2-8-0 No. 48646 gets well away from Dunstable North with a train of coal empties for Leighton Buzzard in lovely low autumn sunshine. Whilst little trace of the previous existence of a railway can be seen here today, the water tower does still exist, and it is not too difficult to locate the exact spot in Drovers Road where the level crossing used to be. Further westward, the alignment down the cutting is now a footpath, although in the opposite direction modern development has made the task of tracing the old track much more difficult.

(*S. Summerson*)

207. High activity at Dunstable North! Still more than 10 years away from final closure, the branch plays host to two 0-6-2Ts as they potter about in the autumn sunshine on Saturday 24 September 1955. On the left N2 No. 69504 has charge of a train of empty coal wagons and centre, N7 No. 69654 approaches the station from across the A5 main road with a passenger train from Luton. One Sunday in July 1969, this bridge, by then cracked and unsafe, was dismantled and removed, Watling Street below being closed to road traffic for the purpose. The site of the station is now occupied by an office block, situated beside the new fire station buildings, and no clue to previous railway occupation remains.

(*H.C. Casserley*)

208. With its train still straddling the A5 below, N7 0-6-2T No. 69631 runs into Dunstable North with what is thought to be the 12.50 train from Luton in May 1959. The driver is occupied at this moment delivering up the single-line token, but the fireman has a very pressing problem to attend to – 'Is the injector working?' he wonders, and leans out of the cab for visual confirmation from underneath.

(Alan Willmott)

209. N2 0-6-2T No. 69582 marshals a short goods train together in Dunstable North Station at 17.00 on Saturday 12 September 1953. Houses along Watling Street (High Street North) peep through in front of the loco, and this tranquil scene was recorded by the photographer half an hour after he had seen the Standard class 4 No. 75034 go through on a Stephenson Locomotive Society special. The branch was quite popular for this purpose in the '50s and early '60s, hosting an interesting variety of motive power, notably that chartered by Brian Lockey for the South Beds Loco Club, and the SLS (see picture 273). *(Harold Clements)*

210. Dominated by the retort house of the local gas works, Dunstable North Station was where (nonsensically) one changed trains when travelling between Luton and Leighton Buzzard – usually. (Some trains were through workings and, of course, there were through excursions, but normally a change here was necessary.) The building between the fruit van and the 'cab' of the push-pull train is the test laboratory, and below it is a row of coal wagons. It is teatime one summer's day in 1955, and 2P 2-6-2T No. 41222 is just leaving for Leighton Buzzard, so the collection of citizenry, if intending to travel, will be waiting to board the train on the right, to Luton. The gas works went when natural gas came, and the whole site fell to modern development after the railway closed in 1966.

(Alan Willmott)

211. Despite the fact that the LNWR had decided that the town of Dunstable was sufficiently important for a branch line to be run there from Leighton Buzzard in 1848, nothing came of suggestions for an easterly connection for a considerable period and, at the time, Lutonians were somewhat miffed by what they considered their less illustrious neighbours beating them in the rail stakes by all of 10 years! Yet it took most of that time before the various warring factions could get their acts together, even though the original proposals for a line to Luton were made as early as 1844. Eventually the first sod was turned at a public ceremony near the Hitchin Road in October 1855, and passenger services commenced along the Dunstable line on 3 May 1858. Although there was no need of major earthworks or expensive constructions to give shareholders headaches, it was decided that the branch should be but a single line, despite connecting with twin tracks at Dunstable. This was a controversial decision at the time, perhaps, but one fully justified later when traffic receipts never really reached expected levels. The original 1855 Parliamentary Act was under the name of 'The Luton, Dunstable & Welwyn Junction Railway', and the line continued south from Luton for its connection with the GN, officially opening on 1 September 1860. But sudden disclosures of debt necessitated a drastic remedy, so almost from the outset, Dunstable was connected to Welwyn (and Hatfield) by the Great Northern Railway, their locomotives being used throughout, and this early view of Dunstable (later, North) Station shows the GN Stirling J4 0-6-0 No. 387 ready to depart with a passenger train for Luton in 1908. The photographer is standing on the bridge across Watling Street, and is looking towards Leighton Buzzard from where the LNWR trains up the branch originate, and on to which through passengers from Luton will have to change. The station building shows that few alterations have taken place during the following 50 years, and in fact the weather-board round the canopy, if unchanged, demonstrates how well preventative maintenance (i.e. painting) was carried out by this one (at least) of the private companies.

(Bernard Matthews Collection)

212. Token changing at Chaul End crossing. Hauling the midday train from Bute Street to Dunstable North, 0-6-2T N7 No. 69639 passes below the elegant GN somersault signal and beside the charming little signal cabin on a sunny Friday 29 May 1956. During World War I a temporary platform was erected here, lasting from March 1916 to February 1920, but today there is a modern concrete bridge across what's left of the railway, taking the road to a roundabout connection with the Luton-Dunstable relief road, thereby connecting Chaul End Lane with Dallow Road.

(S. Summerson)

213. The more you look the more you see! Obviously posed, this wonderfully detailed old photograph of Luton's railway centre, taken early this century, contains a wealth of interesting minutiae, ranging from the old Palace Theatre which stood – until burned down – on the corner of New Bedford Road and Mill Street (top left-hand corner) to a (slightly blurred) MR locomotive passing below the letters 'WARE' of the Midland Railway Goods Warehouse sign (R), and a gentleman in a Luton boater (bottom right-hand corner). But there is so much else on view, including Midland Road (right-centre) and a decorous display of old posters; almost all of it having gone today. Just pore over the picture and appreciate its finer points.

(Luton Museum)

214. You might think, with some justification perhaps, that if you were standing on the London end of the GN platforms in Luton, you would be at the southern end, but you would be wrong, and by the best part of 90° as a glance at the OS map will show. Not that the adjacent Midland Railway cared to be so pedantic – their London-end signal box had been called Luton South since its earliest days, so they didn't mind either what the compass *or* the GN said! Photographers, of course, were totally aware from which direction the sun would be shining and when, knowing full well that at midday here the light would be perfectly suitable for photography, unlike most other Bedfordshire stations where it would be, as they might say, 'up and down the line'. It is for this reason, as much as any, that so many excellent photographs of trains in the Luton area exist, like this fine portrait of N7 0-6-2T No. 69678 passing the accurately-described Luton (Bute Street) East signal box on Tuesday 29 September 1959. Brand new and not yet in use, this flat-topped replacement to the old one (visible above the loco's cab) is about to be commissioned, and was worked until the end of 1969. Just 10 years is not all that much of a life for a new signal box, but it was to be a further nine years, to 1978, before it was finally demolished; still apparently in good nick. The train consists of coal for Luton Gas Works, and since there was no connection with the Midland Main Line here until January 1966, it would have travelled all the way along the branch from Hatfield.

(*S. Summerson*)

215. With its GE Westinghouse pump showing prominently on the right-hand side of its smokebox, 0-6-2T N7 No. 69618 trundles southwards out of Luton Bute Street Station on Saturday 23 May 1959 at the head of a nice long train of wooden-bodied coal empties from Luton Gas Works. Introduced by the Great Eastern Railway in 1914 to an original design, this particular locomotive was actually designated N7/4, of a type introduced in 1940, being a rebuild (with round-topped boiler) of one of the 1914-type machines. Various tinkerings with the class had been taking place since 1925, and by the time Thompson stopped all this in 1943 there had been no less than seven different variants among the 134 examples of the N7 class. Nevertheless they lasted well, and it was not until 1962 that none was left in service – 48 years after the first one appeared; a great testimony to the GE and Hill's sturdy design. No. 69621 has been preserved in working order.

(*S. Summerson*)

216. Country idyll. On leaving their respective stations, the GN branch and the Midland Main Line more or less ran parallel to each other until they were a couple of miles from Harpenden, when the branch swung under the main line and proceeded in a more easterly direction towards Harpenden East, and then across country to join the GN Main Line at Welwyn Junction. This charming country scene was recorded near Luton Hoo, just after the two lines set out on their separate ways, and the Midland Main Line shows clearly above the whole length of the train. The loco, No. 69547, is one of the N2 class of 0-6-2Ts, so often seen on the branch, and sharing most duties with their N7 cousins. This particular version, with short chimney and condensing pipes, was so built for working on the Metropolitan, but other locos (tall chimney, no condenser) and a third variant (short chimney, no condensing equipment) was also at work throughout the GN system. N2 No. 69523 is preserved, and sometimes runs with the number 4744.

(*Peter Waylett*)

THE BEDFORDSHIRE INDUSTRIAL SCENE

217. (top) and 218. (above) Much of Bedfordshire's prosperity this century can be credited directly to the quarry trade, and the biggest employer by far in this industry has been the London Brick Company. With headquarters at Stewartby, the kilns were virtually surrounded by the clay pits, and it was in some of these pits that the steam locos worked. But these were not ordinary steam locos; in fact they were quite extraordinary steam locos. The top picture shows Nos. S1 and S3 at rest while the crews take a tea break, and the bottom picture is a close-up of No. S3, well illustrating the cramped conditions in which the crews operated. Photographed on Saturday 18 April 1953, these unusual 2 ft. 11 in. gauge locos were built six years apart by Sentinel of Shrewsbury; S1 (works No. 7700) in 1929, and S2 (works No. 9221) in 1935. In those pre-inflation days the cost of each was the same – £765 and, weighing all of seven tons, they were rated at 80hp. They only lasted another two years after these photographs were taken, and were sold for scrap in 1955.

(Both pictures: Peter Bland)

219. (above) and 220. (below) These two pictures give some idea of LBC operations at Stewartby round about 1929-30. Above, deep in the pit, the electric navvy (or face shovel) is tipping clay into the hopper for loading into the wagons below. The little Sentinel is not doing too much but, with steam to spare, will have no trouble pushing the wagons out of the pit when they are full. Were the loco to go very far in the opposite direction there would be the likelihood of a fairly big bang because the umbilical power cable to the navvy is draped across the line, and even at only seven tons, the Sentinel would be sure to instigate a ground-level firework display on contact! This pit is now Stewartby Lake. The bottom picture was taken up at the kilns, and the Sentinel is transferring greenbrick (clay) to the furnaces. On emerging after firing, it will be bricks.

(Both pictures: Robin Waywell Collection)

221., 222. and 223. Railway enthusiasts have cause to be very grateful to the Associated Portland Cement Company at Dunstable for two main reasons. First, they operated an extremely interesting stud of steam locomotives which was always accessible to photographers, and second, justification for the Dunstable branch not being lifted when passenger services ceased was to maintain the rail connection into the depot. Not actually situated in Dunstable, the tall chimneys marking the location were really in Houghton Regis, and since long before the last war, the rooftops surrounding the works, because of the continual deposit of chalk dust from above, looked permanently as if they had been snowed upon. There were steam locomotives in the works, and there were steam locomotives in the quarry, three of the latter being captured by the camera of Jim Jarvis when he went there on Saturday 27 August 1938. "Westminster" (above) is the only one still in existence, and is a Peckett 0-6-0ST of 1914. It came second-hand to Houghton Regis, and when no longer required had various homes including a spell on the Kent and East Sussex Railway, but more recently it has been seen at Tistead Station near Alton in Hampshire. The two locos opposite, also 0-6-0STs, were both scrapped. "Edith" (above) was built by Peckett in 1915 and "Eccles" (below) by Manning Wardle in 1894. Like everything else round about, they are covered in chalk dust, but with a good hosing down and a lick of paint, just imagine how they would have been appreciated on a preserved line today. It's wholly possible, though, that the non-standard buffers might have needed modifying before the locos would have been allowed to work any passenger trains!

(All pictures: J.M. Jarvis)

222.

223.

224. (above) and 225. (opposite) To learn that a small, mainly agricultural county such as Bedfordshire has had steam locomotives working on some 20 separate industrial systems over the years may come as quite a surprise to the casual observer, yet recent research by Robin Waywell, the leading expert on local industrial railways, has uncovered this unexpected statistic, and there were once many other lines using different forms of traction or motive power. Of those with steam, two were Air Ministry lines (RAF Henlow and RAF Cardington), the CEGB operated two (Goldington and Little Barford), and Bedford & District Gas Company's own loco shunted their depot. In Luton, Vauxhall Motors worked two lines (one on each side of the Midland), and Laportes had quite an extensive system (off the Dunstable branch) in their Kingsway factory, whilst in Bedford, Howards engineering works had steam locomotives shunting at their premises along the Kempston Road. The remaining railways were all connected with quarrying – cement, sand, lime, stone or clay – but of all these fascinating lines, only one is still in existence; Arnold's sand railway, part of which is preserved and is now known as the Leighton Buzzard Narrow Gauge Railway. This 2 ft. gauge line was officially opened in November 1919, connecting Garside & Arnold's quarries with the Dunstable Branch some four or five miles away, and survived in commercial use for almost 45 years. Both ends of the original line are now gone, but the LBNGR operates passenger trains, usually steam hauled, between the two termini on a regular basis. The picture above shows one of the original Hudson class G 0-6-0WTs on the line, round about 1920, alongside a Bedford-built Simplex petrol loco of 1918. The class G is one of two locomotives built by Hudswell Clarke during World War I for use on the Italian front (works Nos. 1377 and 1378), but they were undelivered by the armistice, and came to Leighton Buzzard in 1919 at a cost of £1,225 each. They were not very successful here, doing little work, and when sold 'as new' some two years later they did not even realise half their purchase price! The picture opposite shows the line in its present form, with the 1877-built 0-4-0 vertical-boilered de Winton locomotive "Chaloner" double-heading with "Peter Pan", a Kerr Stuart 0-4-0ST of 1922. The train is about to cross Appenine Way, Leighton Buzzard, on Saturday 7 September 1991, travelling from Pages Park to Stonehenge.
(Above *Leighton Buzzard Narrow Gauge Railway Society Collection*, Opposite *David Eatwell*)

226. (above) and 227. (opposite) Amongst the many engineering firms which have flourished in Bedford, three of them (quite separately) produced railway vehicles of one sort or another, many of which were exported to work on foreign railways, often in remote corners of the globe. Small diesel (or petrol) shunting locomotives were the prerogative of the Simplex works (see picture 224), but the other two firms were solidly into steam, producing railway cranes of up to 25 tons for systems as diverse as the GWR and Argentine railways. The Bedford Engineering Company in Ampthill Road produced steam cranes for domestic customers (e.g. the London & South Western Railway), and overseas (e.g. Brazil), but closed in 1932, leaving the Vulcan Works along Elstow Road with the sole responsibility for steam crane production in Bedford. It was here, beside the Hitchin line, that Alexander Grafton had set up business in 1886, and steam cranes were produced at this factory until steam went out of fashion, the last models being supplied to BR in 1960. In the interim, Grafton products went as far afield as Paraguay where an old example was still at work at the tannin mill in José Fassardi in August 1994 (above). Domestic railways were also important customers, and large numbers of Grafton cranes were ordered by the Manchester Sheffield & Lincolnshire Railway, the London Brighton & South Coast Railway and BR. The picture opposite shows a preserved example demonstrating its prowess at a wet open-day in Chatham Docks on Sunday 25 November 1984, with the Robert Stephenson & Hawthorn 0-4-0ST "Ajax" of 1941 doing a bit of shunting behind. The similarity between these two standard gauge steam cranes is immediately apparent (despite the Paraguay model having been modified to improve the air conditioning!) as Alexander Grafton's original design was so good that it was hardly necessary to change it other than in detail during the 74 years of manufacture. What a tribute to a great engineer.

(Above *Ray Schofield*, Opposite *David Eatwell*)

228. (above) and 229. (below) The Marston Valley Brick Company's lines were the most extensive of all the Bedfordshire brickworks, yet away from base they did not employ any locomotives after the early '50s. What they used was a cable-operated tramway, very similar in principle to the San Francisco cable cars, to fetch in the clay from the pits, and the tramlines were a familiar scene in mid-Bedfordshire for many years. They were 2 ft. 6 in. gauge and lasted right up to 1978 when the much simpler conveyor belt system supplanted them. The picture above shows what later became the Shanks & McEwan landfill site at the bottom of Brogborough Hill, looking north, and the picture below is of the brick-built gantry at Ridgmont. Although the brickworks are now demolished, close inspection of the area will reveal much evidence in the form of cuttings, bridges, etc. of these interesting and lengthy railway lines, which local lads often used (illegally, but excitingly) to hitch a ride around the fields. When apprehended, the lads would make off in different directions to the annoyance of staff who were never known actually to catch a young offender! Perhaps they never really tried. *(Both pictures: Robin Leleux)*

230. (above) and 231. (below) Vauxhall Motors, at their plant in Luton, have had the use of three steam locos in their own private sidings, and two of these attractive little shunters are illustrated. Photographed on Tuesday 1 November 1948, the picture above is of a Peckett 0-4-0ST, Works No. 1874, of 1936, as immaculately turned out as any loco could possibly be, with its Peckett-built hand lamp still gracing the top lamp-bracket. No. 1874 was eventually replaced by a diesel shunter (how *could* they?) and was later sold for work in a Norfolk sand quarry. In far less glamorous condition (below) is "C.J. Wills" an 0-6-0ST by Hudswell Clarke (Works No. 671 of 1904) which came second-hand from a firm of contractors in 1941. It lasted until scrapping round about 1950. The third loco at Vauxhall's was the Manning Wardle 0-4-0ST "Kitchener" of 1915, but it was only here for a short period on loan in 1953.   (*Both pictures: Harold Clements*)

232. (top) and 233. (bottom) Goldington Power Station lasted less than 30 years, following which time memories of thick black smoke constantly belching from the chimneys caused many people to say 'And a good job, too,' but it was an unmissable landmark during its stay, and a stirling employer to a large number of Bedfordians. The boilers burnt coal – well, coal dust really – and at the time of construction in the early-'50s a new siding off the Bedford-Sandy line was put in for the regular delivery of coal. Even after the rest of the Cambridge line had been closed, this section from St John's was retained just to keep the generating station supplied with fuel, but during the late '70s these deliveries were switched to road, and a short time later the success of nuclear power elsewhere sounded the death knell for installations such as Goldington. Before construction, the site was a lovely green meadow down by the river. Today it is a modern housing estate with adjacent supermarket. That's progress? There were six steam locomotives here, five Andrew Barclays and a Robert Stephenson & Hawthorn, but it was rare for more than two locomotives to be working at any one time; one of the AB's being for spares. ED9, immediately recognisable as a product of the Kilmarnock factory, was built in 1954, works No. 2352, and was delivered new to Goldington. When redundancy fell, the preservation movement was well established and there was no question of the 0-4-0ST being broken up. Instead, ED9, not in working order, has travelled around the south of England looking for a home, but after reposing for a while in a children's playground, seems to be much more settled with the Swindon & Cricklade preservation group that has now be-friended it. These two pictures were taken on Thursday 3 April 1969. (*Both pictures: David Eatwell*)

234. Like "Westminster" from Houghton Regis and ED9 from Goldington, "GF No. 3" from Laportes in Luton may still be seen today, as it also was saved for preservation when its days of gainful employment were deemed to be over. Built by Andrew Barclay of Kilmarnock in 1916, works No. 1477, this 0-4-0 fireless locomotive was manufactured for military use at the Gretna Factory in Scotland and was their number three, hence the number plate. "GF No. 3" arrived at Laporte's factory in Luton round about 1936 and stayed there until it went to Quainton Road, near Aylesbury, for preservation in 1971. Fireless locomotives were dependent on using an outside steam supply, so could not venture very far from base, and without a conventional chimney and (often) cylinders under the cab, the overall appearance was, to say the least, different, as can be seen in this remarkable old pre-war picture. *(Harold Clements)*

235. Industrial railways and their locomotives have always been something of a minority interest in this country but, like foreign railways, they have their aficianados who devote much energy to the pursuit of their hobby. Throughout the world, where there were railways, there were industrial railways, but as in Britain most of them are no more. Three or four important concentrations of industrial railways using steam are still extant abroad – the sugar railways of Cuba, Java, the Philippines and the forest railways of Romania are about the lot – but at home the vast majority have fallen by the wayside. Even in their heyday they were in the main hidden away in coal mines, quarries, steel works, gas works and factories, but a small band of experts did manage to penetrate many industrial steam strongholds with their notebooks and cameras. One such reasonably accessible location was the quarry belonging to the Totternhoe Lime and Stone Company, not far from Dunstable. There were Sentinels here (two still exist), Manning Wardles and locos built by Peckett, Robert Stephenson & Hawthorn, and an Avonside which was saved from the breaker's torch by the Colne Valley Railway in Essex. And there was this wonderful Aveling & Porter (one of a pair). Really nothing more than a traction engine on rails, it was built in 1927, works No. 11087, and came new to Totternhoe at that time, performing well until being scrapped on site around 1943. The picture was taken in 1936.   (*J.M. Jarvis*)

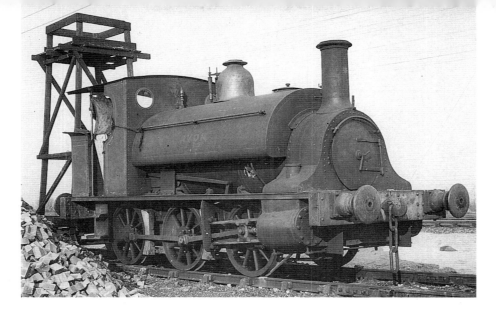

236. (above) and 237. (below) The Coronation Brickworks of the Bedford Brick Company were some three or four miles south of Bedford at a location known generally by the name of the nearby pub – Chimney Corner – and of all the brickworks in Bedfordshire, this was the only one to have a standard gauge railway working from an overhead electricity supply. There was no non-electrified portion, yet locomotives by Aveling & Porter and Sentinel worked on it, as did a most attractive outside cylindered 0-6-0ST named "Avon". Built by Fox Walker of Bristol in 1877 (works No. 328), "Avon" (above) came second-hand from a firm in Greenwich, and the photographer recounts the story of how he was travelling north on the Midland Main Line on Saturday 18 April 1936 when he spotted the loco from his train window, was so surprised to see it here that he alighted at Bedford, made his way back to Chimney Corner and photographed "Avon" (with the maintenance trolley for the overhead wires behind). The loco was only here 12 months, leaving later in 1936, and it must be wondered whether its braking system (note the wooden brake blocks) had anything to do with such a short residency. But on the overhead system the loco in use was "Ruth" (below). Built by English Electric in 1935 (works No. 899), the Bedford Brick Company was its first owner and it stayed here all its working life. "Ruth" was scrapped in 1971, but not before going through various colour changes – green when new, then yellow, and finally a dull red for the last 10 years of its life. Although quite basic in design, "Ruth" worked well on the 500v DC system, developing 60 hp to the 3 ft. 2 in. driving wheels, and was able to reach all of 8.3 mph! The photograph shows it under the wires at the Coronation works on Saturday 18 April 1953 (exactly 17 years to the day after "Avon" above), and note the signal gantry on the right indicating activity pending on both down lines of the Midland Main Line.

(Above *J.M. Jarvis*, Below *Peter Bland*)

'Pleasure' Railways

238. Whipsnade Zoo (now more politically correctly named 'Whipsnade Wildlife Park') has had a 2 ft. 6 in. gauge railway operating within its precincts since the early '70s, by which visitors can be transported right through the rhino compound and inaccessible paddocks in comfort and safety aboard one of the specially built coaches on the Whipsnade & Umfolozi Railway (the rhinos came from Umfolozi). The first such train ran on Thursday 26 August 1971, consisting of five coaches and the steam locomotive "Chevalier". One man's gain is another man's loss, as they say, and Whipsnade would not have a railway (at least not *this* one) if it hadn't been for Bowaters deciding to abandon their industrial railway at Sittingbourne, Kent, in favour of road transport at just the right time (1969), thereby releasing their locomotives and certain items of rolling stock for relocation. The much reduced system is now run by a preservation group, whilst the other major 2 ft. 6 in. gauge railway in Britain is the Welshpool & Llanfair Light Railway in Wales, and there has already been a certain amount of interchange of vehicles between the two latter organisations, so it would not be impossible to see locomotives from one of these lines working on the other, perhaps in friendly exchange or in an emergency. Four ex-Bowaters locos came to Whipsnade, and some goods wagons, the chassis of which were used in the construction of the ten new coaches in which passengers ride. The picture above shows the oldest loco to come from Bowaters, the smart little 1908-built "Excelsior", a 0-4-0ST by Kerr Stuart, at work at Whipsnade on Sunday 17 September 1978. Loco and train wait in the new station for passengers to board.   (*David Eatwell*)

239. "Excelsior" (*see* opposite) runs through the white rhino paddock at Whipsnade Zoo with its complement of three special coaches on a sunny Sunday in September 1978 without so much as a hint of acknowledgement from the grazing rhinoceros. *(David Eatwell)*

240. For 16 years (from 1974 to 1990) Whipsnade played host to a most surprising item of ironmongery – the ex-Zambesi Saw Mills Railway 7th class 4-8-0 No. 390. Artist, conservationist and steam enthusiast David Shepherd came across the loco at the ZSM headquarters in Livingstone, Zambia, in 1971 and had it brought back to England in full working order. But, as the southern African standard gauge is 3 ft. 6 in., there was nowhere here for No. 390 to run! This problem was eventually solved by the laying of a short length of track adjacent to the Whipsnade & Umfolozi Railway to accommodate both loco and the 1927 sleeping-car that David acquired at the same time. Built by Sharp Stewart of Glasgow in 1896, No. 390 is a wood-burner, as one would expect of a loco working on a saw-mill factory line, and on special occasions it could be steamed during its stay at Whipsnade. This was as much for the delight of the staff as for the entertainment of visitors, since 10 yards was about the maximum distance it could travel before falling off the end of the specially laid line! Just such a steaming was taking place on Friday 25 July 1986, but it was a comparatively rare occurrence, and not long after this the boiler certificate ran out, making further steamings impossible. Since 1990, our only wood-burning 4-8-0, the coach and other ZSM railwayana have moved down to David's main centre of activity, the East Somerset Railway at Cranmore near Shepton Mallet in Somerset, and it seems unlikely that this wonderful old example of Victorian technology can be seen at work in the foreseeable future, but it *is* on static display, and the usual warm welcome is always afforded visitors who take the trouble to travel to the ESR. See you there, perhaps.

(*David Eatwell*)

241. At the same time that No. 390 (opposite) was being steamed, the Locomotive Club of Great Britain (Bedford Branch) was holding a special evening steaming at Whipsnade with members and their families enjoying almost unlimited travel round the circuit, until darkness brought things to a close. The loco chosen for use that day was "Superior", a 1920-built Kerr Stuart 0-6-2T which came to Whipsnade from Bowaters in 1970. The condition of the locos here is nothing short of immaculate, and "Superior", built as an oil-burner but later modified to coal firing, is graced by the 'LCGB Bedford' headboard as passengers take their places for yet another round trip. *(David Eatwell)*

242. (above) and 243. (opposite) One of the least known steam railways of Bedfordshire must have been the 1 ft. 11^1/$_2$ in. gauge pleasure line that was constructed in the grounds of Woburn Abbey in the late 1960s. Coinciding almost exactly with steam's final fling on Britain's main lines, Woburn Park Railway carried its first passengers on Sunday 3 March 1968, but it was another five weeks before a steam locomotive arrived (on Sunday 7 April) and the railway started operating in earnest over the Easter holiday the following weekend. Ex-Dinorwic Quarries "No. 1" has the works No. 1429 and was built in 1922, coming direct to Woburn following overhaul at Gowers in Wilstead, to work on the line started by Trevor Barber and some friends from the Vauxhall motor works in Luton. Unfortunately, for various reasons, the life of the railway was very short and, following its closure, "No. 1" went to work on the Knebworth & Wintergreen Light Railway in nearby Hertfordshire. (The present railway in the Safari Park uses steam-outline diesel locomotives and is in a completely different position.) The picture above shows the 0-4-0ST soon after its arrival at Woburn, and opposite, it can be seen working in the grounds of Knebworth House on Saturday 24 July 1976, double-headed with the late Rev. Teddy Boston's 1919 Bagnall-built 0-4-0ST "Pixie".

(Above *Colin Smith*, Opposite *David Eatwell*)

AROUND THE COUNTY

244. Few days could be spent linesiding at venues such as Sandy and Hitchin in the 1920s and '30s without seeing a 'Ragtimer'. These two-cylindered Gresley K2 Moguls were notorious for rough riding, and thus gained their nickname from an energetic dance rhythm of around 70 years ago. They were, however, reliable mixed-traffic engines and, despite originating as early as 1912 (they were Gresley's first all-new design), the entire class of 75 survived to enter BR service in 1948 with many still earning a crust in the early 1960s. No. 4681 – seen here whipping a typical mixed goods train along the fast line at Sandy on Saturday 1 May 1937 – belonged to a batch of 25 built by Kitson & Co., of Leeds. In the 1930s several K2s were transferred to Scotland and received the names of Highland lochs, but No. 4681 (BR No. 61771) remained south of the border and was therefore never honoured with such an embellishment.

(*Les Hanson*)

245. A typically filthy Standard class 4 on the St John's line! Between this point and Sandy it has been single track all the way (apart from the station passing loops), and as soon as the fireman of No. 75036 has relinquished the token at the approaching Bedford St John's No. 2 signal box, he and his train will regain double track for the run into the station over the last mile of this leisurely ramble from Cambridge. The River Great Ouse at this point was always a popular place for swimming, and to spend a warm summer's afternoon along this stretch of water was the favoured activity of many a young trainspotter of the day. When this photograph was taken on Saturday 12 July 1958, the Newnham Swimming Pool was still packing 'em in at the picturesque setting the other side of the line, and it was always reckoned to be a good test of a spotter if he could see the number of a passing loco between the trunks of the tall poplar trees from there. Newnham Baths have disappeared under the car park of the Aspects Leisure Centre, the bridge is now a footpath with all other signs of the railway long gone, but the river is still pretty well unchanged, as are the poplar trees, and the young trainspotters of the '40s and '50s will look at scenes like this to be transported back to those halcyon days when all that seemed to matter was whether the next loco along would be a 'cop' or not. It may not be fashionable to dwell on the past, but where would we be without our memories?   (Peter Waylett)

246. Real drama! No. 47995 was one of the 33 Beyer Garratt 2-6-0+0-6-2 articulated locomotives introduced in 1927 to work heavy coal trains on the LMS, but they were never as successful as had been hoped, being generally OK when just out-shopped, yet quickly deteriorating with mileage. They were fine looking machines, as can be seen, implying high power, but restrictive design features forced upon the manufacturers by the LMS reduced the locomotives' overall effectiveness and, although they lasted in service for about 30 years, they did nothing to enhance Beyer Peacock's reputation in this country. With the end of its long train still in Ampthill Tunnel, No. 47995 is heading for Brent with coal from Toton on a winter's afternoon in the early '50s, the driver clearly enjoying the fresh air and sunshine.

(*Norman E. Stead*)

247. (left) Ivatt's large-boilered Great Northern Atlantics were the mainstay of the express services out of King's Cross to the north prior to the Gresley A1s (later A3s) coming on stream in the 1920s. The C1 4-4-2s continued to give sterling service throughout the 1930s, and it was here at Sandy that we see No. 4457 rushing through with a northbound express on Saturday 1 May 1937. Of 93 such locos built between 1902 and 1910, 17 of the class were still in service at nationalisation in 1948, but within two years the lot had been withdrawn. They were all broken up, except No. 251 which survives to be seen in the National Collection at York Museum (see picture 264).

(*Les Hanson*)

248. (right) 4F 0-6-0 No. 44175 ambles past Luton's Crescent Road Yard on the southbound slow line and heads towards Harpenden with maybe a shunting session at St Albans to follow. A scan of this panoramic view of south central Luton reveals many landmarks which are as much a part of history today as is the very concept of this nice little goods train. The huge cooling towers have thankfully disappeared, and so has the antiquated power station which necessitated their presence – it being one of the last left in the country to supply DC mains for domestic use. Pondswick Road houses (left) are gone, too, and during a short period after the site was cleared, but before development took place a big top was erected here in which various events were held, one of the most memorable being the appearance of Lionel Hampton and his Big Band in concert. If you were there, I'm sure *you'll* never forget it either.

(*S. Summerson*)

249. One of the huge LMS-designed 2-6-0+0-6-2 Beyer Garratts of the late '20s, No. 47994, passes mile-post 29 by the sprawling Vauxhall Motors works at Luton with a long train predominantly of coal wagons on the afternoon of Monday 9 May 1955. Despite being a little uneconomical on fuel, and with an inherent unreliability problem, these massive machines continued to be turned out by Toton Motive Power Depot to haul the heavyweight coal trains to London until gradually the LMS Stanier 2-8-0 8Fs and the highly versatile Standard class 9F 2-10-0s took command. No. 47994 covered 584,200 miles during a lifespan of about 30 years, and as this relates to an average of less than 19,500 miles per annum, it is not difficult to understand why the LMS Garratts were not regarded as particularly successful locomotives.

(Harold Clements)

250. (right) A page from a working timetable of September 1954.
(*Chris Foren Collection*)

251. (below) Setting back into the down platform at Hitchin, Ivatt class 2MT 2-6-2T No. 41329 will soon have a few passengers in its single coach for the return trip along the branch back home to Bedford, having spent most of the time since its arrival in the sidings immediately north of the platforms. This versatile 2MT locomotive had the distinction of being the last-built of a class which numbered a total of 130, and upon closure of the Hitchin branch to passenger services from Saturday 30 December 1961, it was transferred to continue its useful work on the Southern Region.
(*L. King*)

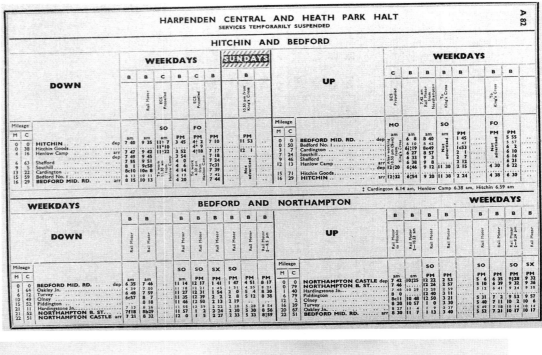

252. Wainwright P class 0-6-0T 'Bluebell' (in blue), Deepdale, Potton, July 1983.

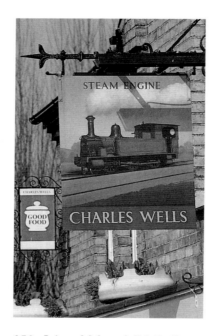

253. Isle of Man, MN Railway 0-6-0T 'Caledonia' (in red), Arlesey, April 1983.

254. MR Johnson 2-4-0 (in green), Bedford, April 1983.

255. Sharp Stewart Furness Railway E1 2-4-0 of 1870 (in faded red), Ampthill, May 1983.

252. to 259. The study of pub signs is called 'hostelaphilly' (according to Collins Encyclopaedia), so perhaps the study of those featuring steam locomotives might be called 'ferro-equine-hostelaphilly'! But, pub signs *do* attract interest, particularly with regard to the accuracy (or inaccuracy, as in the case of the sign for the Great Northern in Bute Street, Luton – see opposite) of the artist's portrayal. Have you noticed, for example, that outside-cylinder locomotives rarely appear on pub signs, and that when they do the artist has generally hidden the mechanical detail behind a plume of escaping steam! Shown above and opposite is a selection of local pub signs that are no more – they have either been replaced by different pictures or, in the case of Bedford's Midland Hotel, the building has changed its use and name. The dates given are when each sign was photographed, and the captions refer to what the artist *might* have been intending. (All pictures *David Eatwell*)

256. Stirling Single(!) (in green), Bute Street, Luton, May 1983.

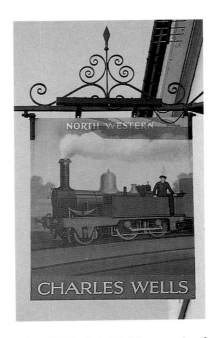

257. GWR 2-4-0T Metrotank of the 1870s (in green with red under-frames), Wolverton, July 1984.

258. LMS 0-6-0 4F, St John's, Bedford, June 1984.

259. LMS 0-6-0 4F St John's, Bedford, June 1984.

261. An early Midland bridge notice of 1875, photographed on 6 June 1962 near Leagrave. *(S. Summerson)*

260. A pair of Black Fives occupy the tracks at the north end of Wellingborough Station – No. 45274 of Cricklewood coming in for the stop with a St Pancras express, and an unidentified loco coming out of the carriage sidings on the right. Dominating the scene, though, is the Victorian lodging house, so well remembered by so many railwaymen with such a variety of emotions. The Hilton it was not, nor even home from home, but after a hard trip in from depots like Westhouses or Canklow, Toton or Hasland, footplate crews were only too pleased to book in to the spartan conditions for an uncomfortable bed and the legendary Wellingborough sausages, before working back on their next tour of duty. Wellingborough Lodging House closed in 1961, but lodging turns had been a way of life for as long as anyone could remember, and with their demise another long-established feature of railway life came to an end. *(John Harrison)*

262. Illuminated certificate presented to Bill Garner in recognition of his services as Chairman of the Bedford Branch of ASLEF, 1935-1938.
(Courtesy: *John and Stella Garner*)

SOME SPECIALS

263. Saturday 5 October 1963 was the day that the 'Wandering 1500' came through Bedford on its mammoth 233-mile day-excursion. Based on Broad Street, the special carried M&GNJR Society members through Finsbury Park, Hitchin, Bedford, Northampton, Blisworth, Stratford-upon-Avon, Hatton, Rugby and Willesden before depositing the train-load of satisfied passengers back where they started, but many hours later. The loco used throughout was the Holden GE B12 4-6-0 No. 61572 of 1928, the last of its class in service, and on this occasion in steam for the very last time for BR. When the North Norfolk Railway became established at Sheringham, a home for No. 61572 was found there, and following complete restoration, mainly at a factory in the former East Germany, the B12 was returned to steam at the end of 1994. Here it passes over the River Great Ouse, soon after crossing the Bletchley line on the flat at St John's. (S. Summerson)

264. One of the best remembered rail excursions to pass through Bedfordshire was the 'Plant Centenarian', run to celebrate the 100th birthday of Doncaster Works on Sunday 27 September 1953. Double-headed Atlantics hauled the lengthy train up the East Coast Main Line to King's Cross: the 1898-built No. 990 "Henry Oakley" leading and No. 251 of 1902 as the train engine. What a combination, and one that might still be repeated, given a little goodwill, as both locos have been preserved at the NRM – "Henry Oakley" having already been returned to steam once and used on the Keighley & Worth Valley Railway for a short period in the late '70s. For the 'Plant Centenarian', the obvious intention was to give participants a good run for their money, and two of the Eastern Region's top link men were in charge: Ted Hailstone on "Henry Oakley" and Bill Hoole on No. 251. That they were demanding (and getting!) maximum effort from their firemen is obvious in this view of the train rushing over Cadwell Crossing, Ickleford, just north of Hitchin, when as long ago as 1953, an event such as this was able to attract interested spectators to such relatively remote locations. *(Harold Clements)*

265. When the museum of British Transport at Clapham (south London) closed in the early '70s, the contents were dispersed, and many of the larger exhibits were put in store pending relocation. At about the same time it was decided that, as the 1927 Railway Museum in Queen Street, York, could not be extended to house any more locomotives, it should be moved to the redundant York shed, where many more items could be put on show. The new title was to be the National Railway Museum, with the entrance in Leeman Road, as indeed both still are today. HRH the Duke of Edinburgh performed the opening ceremony on Saturday 27 September 1975, but it was very much an embryo concern at first, mainly built around the engines which had come from the old Queen Street Museum. As Leeman Road became able to take more locomotives, some from Clapham (plus one or two others that were being kept in the south of England) were moved north down the Midland Main Line, some in 1975 and others in 1977. All the movements took place on Saturdays with a very severe speed restriction and frequent inspection stops, the trains carrying railway police for security reasons, with crews aboard 'selected' locos to lubricate and check for hot-boxes en route. Two of these transfers are shown (above and opposite) coming through Bedford. Here "Mallard" (note 'rider'!) and the LSWR Adams 4-4-0 T3 No. 563 of 1893 (coupled to the tender of GER No. 490) pass under Ford End Road bridge and run into Bedford Midland Road Station on 12 April 1975.

(David Eatwell)

266. On 19 April 1975 it was the turn of the Midland Compound No. 1000 to go north (with bird droppings soiling the shining boiler!), travelling behind the 1904-built GE 0-6-0T No. 87, seen here at Bedford. The building behind the Compound is the original Midland engine shed, or what was left of it after it had been shortened in 1956 and turned into a workshop. Prior to that it was a wagon store, but another claim to fame was that for a time during World War II it housed the experimental red and white streamlined diesel rail-car (shown in picture 198).

(*David Eatwell*)

267. It was not really the vogue to start using selected locomotives on special trains until the 1950s, so pre-war events of this type were fairly few and far between. One notable special, and one of which some of the earliest colour photographs of a train in motion were taken, was the Stirling Single No. 1's return trip along the East Coast Main Line between King's Cross and Peterborough on Sunday 11 September 1938. Not in service at this time but kept for 'special events', No. 1 was built in 1870 and retired in 1907, so was approaching its 70th birthday when it undertook this amiable public appearance. Now part of the NRM collection, the beautiful 4-2-2 was restored to working order under their auspices in the early 1980s and was sometimes to be seen on preserved lines hauling two or three coaches for a filming project, perhaps, or for 'educational' purposes, but only on a very limited number of occasions has it been allowed to take fare-paying passengers for a ride. The picture shows the 1938 special pausing at Hitchin on the way back to King's Cross with, surprisingly perhaps for the time, a group of interested onlookers.

(Harold Clements)

268. (main) and 269. (inset) On a national basis, the Locomotive Club of Great Britain has long been in the forefront of running special trains both at home and abroad, and today is probably best known for its overseas tours which visit all parts of the world where there are railways. In the '60s, however, much of its energy was directed towards the domestic market, and LCGB rail-tours ran all over the British Isles, many of them through our own county. Not many specials actually originated in Bedford, but one that did was the LCGB South Midlands Rail Tour of Saturday 17 October 1964, giving locals a rare treat by starting at Midland Road Station. Motive power for the main part of the trip was Willesden's Black Five No. 45292, and the route adopted was to Wolverton (via Swanbourne Sidings and the Bletchley Flyover), the Newport Pagnall branch (using the Fairburn 2-6-4T No. 42105), Northampton, Market Harborough, and back to Bedford up the Midland Main Line through Wellingborough and, most unusually, Sharnbrook Tunnel. What a bonus! The main picture on this page shows the 4-6-0 sitting at the head of its train in the Hitchin bay awaiting departure from Bedford, and later (inset) the Fairburn is seen passing sedately through New Bradwell on the Newport Pagnall branch. (Main picture *Dave Mills*; inset *Peter Waylett*)

270. to 273. The Stephenson Locomotive Society ran a very popular special on Saturday 14 April 1962, and no wonder it was so popular, in view of the route chosen and the locomotives utilised. Departing Birmingham in the morning, the SLS Special was hauled by LMS class 2 4-4-0 No. 40646 to Northampton, where Fowler 2-6-2T No. 40026 was coupled inside for the 20-mile run along the branch to Bedford, when the class 2 came off to run light-engine to Luton Bute Street. In order to be right way round for the return, No. 40646 had to travel to Bletchley where it turned, ran tender-first to Leighton Buzzard and through Dunstable to Luton. In the meantime, the train, behind No. 40026, was travelling along another branch to Hitchin, and here, 0-6-0ST J52 No. 1247, resplendent in its GN livery, was waiting to do more branch-line work, this time Hatfield to Bute Street. With No. 40646 now ready to resume duty, the special returned direct to Leighton Buzzard, then down the WCML to Birmingham, and the pictures on these two pages show various stages of the day's events. Above, No. 40026 is heading for Hitchin on the double-line section at Ireland (between Southill and Shefford) and below, No. 40646 (with No. 1247 at the other platform) is waiting to leave Bute Street. On the right (above), No. 1247 takes water, also at Bute Street, and below, No. 40646 hurries through Stanbridgeford Station on the return to Birmingham. Such complicated workings would be regarded as impossible to organise today, wouldn't they? But, with a little bit of imagination …

(Top left *Peter Waylett*; below left and top right *Harpenden Railway Museum Collection*; below right *Peter Waylett*)

274. Many specials are unadvertised, 'hush-hush' affairs, and one such went through Bedford early on Saturday morning, 30 March 1974, when Mr William McAlpine's much loved locomotive "Flying Scotsman" travelled south down the Midland Main Line from Market Overton, on to the St John's triangle and over the branch to Bletchley where it was to be on show for a couple of days in connection with the winding-up of the old Bletchley Town Council. In Bedford's very foggy conditions, speed was in region of 5 mph, so photographers found keeping up to be no problem, and amazingly, for just a few minutes, they were rewarded when the mists cleared for the arrival at St John's No. 1 signal box. "Flying Scotsman" is seen here with its extra tender and short train of privately-owned coaches just coming out from under Ampthill Road bridge, the same location as No. 45147 in picture 193.

(*David Eatwell*)

275. and 276. It didn't take long for local trainspotters to hear about the arrival from Glasgow of the Highland Railway's 1893-built 'Jones Goods' on Bedford shed early in May 1964. The grapevine was just as active then as it is today, although were No. 103 to appear suddenly on a provincial town shed in England now, nobody would be able to get past the army of guards protecting it! The news soon spread that the big yellow 4-6-0 was going to be in filming sequences for *Those Magnificent Men in Their Flying Machines* along the recently closed Hitchin branch, and photographers were out in force 'assisting' the cameramen from Gaumont British. No. 103 had arrived on Thursday 7 May under its own steam, complete with Scottish crews, and the first task to be undertaken was a certain amount of repainting to pretend that the loco was French! (It's a constant source of amusement to enthusiasts seeing locomotives and trains in films and on TV, as very rarely do producers go to the trouble of bothering about 'minor' details like authenticity or accuracy! In films, it seems, a train is a train is a train. In this film, as well as a totally unsuitable locomotive, another comical clanger is the appearance of Goldington Power Station's cooling towers and chimneys above No. 103 in one aerial shot which, since the story is set at the turn of the century, is as unlikely to be accurate as No. 103 is likely to be French!) For the filming, the word 'NORD' was painted on the right-hand-side only of the tender, but in the smaller picture on this page showing the locomotive inside Bedford shed on Saturday 9 May, it is just the trestle which gives any clue as to what is about to happen. In the larger picture the tender has been 'suitably' decorated, and an addition to the roof of the second coach shows where Terry Thomas 'landed' his plane before it crashed into the north portal of Old Warden Tunnel. In this picture, showing the train passing Ireland on the way to Shefford at the end of a day's filming, it seems that the locomotive has had some quite heavy use, judging by the burns that have appeared on the smokebox door! After more than a fortnight at Bedford, the excitement ended here at 07.35 on Monday 25 May when No. 103 set off to return to Scotland, again under its own steam.

(*Small picture S. Summerson, larger picture Peter Waylett*)

277. Mystery picture. Obviously the south end of Luton's Midland Road Station, and obviously a Caprotti class 5 locomotive, but when was it photographed and where was it going? No prizes for the answers, but a pat on the back if you know. *(Dave Mills Collection)*

278. And finally – live steam came back to Bedford shed (briefly) on two nights in December 1990, but few were here to see it! Black Five No. 44932 and Standard class 4 No. 80080 were in steam but were being hauled by a diesel from their home at the Midland Railway Centre, Butterley to St Pancras for a filming assignment, the London terminus (or part of it) being transformed into Zürich Hbf for the day. Sitting in front of the old Midland shed at 01.00, the two locomotives made as nostalgic a sight as had been seen at Bedford since the early '60s, but pictures like this would not have been possible without the considerable help and co-operation of BR's Customer Services Manager (St Pancras) Malcolm Burgoyne and the Bedford train crews who arranged for the diesel to be uncoupled and shifted out of the shot for the few minutes it took this time-exposure photograph to be taken. On reaching London, the locomotives were 'decorated' to masquerade as Austrian wartime engines for scenes in the 20th Century Fox feature film *Shining Through*, starring Michael Douglas and Melanie Griffith, but if you remember the film you won't remember the St Pancras (Zürich Hbf) scenes because they ended up on the cutting-room floor at a reported wasting of £100,000! The original choice of loco had apparently been No. 46203 "Princess Margaret Rose" (one wonders whether 20th Century Fox thought that a red Pacific looked more Austrian than a Black Five or a Standard class 4), but it seems that BR vetoed this, saying that the Princess Royal was too heavy, and what would have been the first visit of a member of this class to St Pancras did not in fact occur. At the time of writing, momentous changes are taking place on Britain's railways, and things thought impossible only a short time ago are happily occurring on a regular basis, but nothing can ever replace the atmospheric sights and smells of steam railways as they once were, so we are left to enjoy the ersatz in the absence of the authentic. Nostalgia may be a thing of the past, but without it many of us would be unable to face the future, and this collection of photographs, I hope, will prove to be lastingly therapeutic.

(David Eatwell)

INDEX